The HyperDoc Handbook

Digital Lesson Design Using Google Apps

Lisa Highfill   Kelly Hilton   Sarah Landis

The HyperDoc Handbook

© 2016 by Lisa Highfill, Kelly Hilton, Sarah Landis

These books are available at special discounts when purchased in quantity for use as premiums, promotions, fundraising and educational use. For inquiries and details, contact the publisher: ElevateBooksEdu.com.

Published by Elevate Books EDU
Paperback ISBN: 978-1-7336468-9-5
Ebook ISBN: 978-1-7334814-0-3

Contents

Foreword
Why We Need to Change How We Learn

High school senior Jordan Moldenhauer shares a student perspective
about being a modern student in a traditional classroom:

As a high-school student, school is the most stressful part of my life, and that's how it should be. I should care about what I am learning and how it affects my future. I should be nervous when I turn in a big paper because I know it matters to me. I don't have a problem with working hard in school, because it does matter. It matters because I am going to college in a year. It matters because after college I am going to be a teacher. And it matters because I will need to have a passion for what I am learning so I can instill that love of learning in the kids I teach.

But sometimes it feels like I'm not learning.

To me, learning is an exploration of the topics that I have a passion for, am curious about, or haven't heard of yet. Instead of learning, though, school is a place where I am told what to do, when to do it, and how to do it—down to a T. It has gotten to the point that, when my teacher tells the class how to do a project, students near me ask, "Can I do this? What about this?" or, "Is it okay if I do this?" But I don't think you should have to ask. We have forgotten what it's like to learn and have instead taken to mindless note-taking and reading PowerPoints and hours of homework, all for a letter on a piece of paper to show people we are good enough to go to their college or work for their company. If we have to ask a teacher if something is okay, we have forgotten how to be creative and are afraid to be creative because we are afraid of being wrong.

If old adages tell us we learn from our mistakes, our teachers should help us understand the same. But we should also understand that a different way of thinking isn't wrong. I think teachers can often inhibit our thinking by inhibiting their own. They have a set understanding of how they want things to go instead of an open mind of where they could go. Instead of possibilities, they want results.

I take AP classes, and I love them. So obviously, something must have gone right, meaning the whole system isn't a disaster. But instead of being told what to do and when to do it, I would love to be given something to learn about and then do it myself. I don't want to be told what to think; I want to be given facts that can help me think for myself. And when I form an opinion, I want my teachers to have the courage to hear me out, not tell me I am wrong. Trust me, it has happened; and I regret to say that I think it will happen in the future.

School is stressful, and it should be. I get good grades. They look great on paper, but is the stress worth it if the only thing I have to show is a diploma? College is where free thinkers blossom, but freethinking shouldn't start in college. And sometimes "traditional teaching methods" prevent me from seeing the current world. My favorite teacher told me, "The difference between school and life is that in school, you're given the lesson to take the test, and in life, you're given the test that teaches you a lesson." It wouldn't be fair to say I want to take a test before I know the material, but doesn't it make sense to teach us with experience rather than words? Teach me what I need to know, but also teach me how to figure it out. The real world isn't about what's going to be on the test. The real world is a test. And we are all taking it.

HyperDocs
The Ultimate Change Agent

We want our students to be creative, collaborative, critical thinkers and communicators—and then we ask them to sit quietly while we explain everything and tell them exactly how to do a task. School doesn't have to be this way, and if we want to prepare students for life in the twenty-first century, it *shouldn't* be.

As a result of the implementation of Google Apps for Education, a new world of opportunities opened up for a shift in the student classroom experience. If used effectively, these tools provide students opportunities to critically think, create, collaborate, and connect in this fast-paced world. Gone are the days of students learning information solely from their teachers. In today's world, every student who has the access, knowledge, skills, will, and capacity has the potential to learn anything that they want to learn.

Students are curious by nature; we just need to provide opportunities for them to be curious. They are amazing problem solvers when we give the opportunity to create information, rather than consume it, and to talk to one another, rather than sit and passively listen. They just need inspiration.

Enter the ultimate change agent in the blended learning classroom: HyperDocs—transformative, interactive Google Docs that replace the standard worksheet method of delivering instruction. We invented the term HyperDoc to describe the digital lesson design and delivery of instruction that was happening in our classrooms. A HyperDoc is the teaching pedagogy involved when making important decisions about what to teach and how to teach with technology to redefine the overall student experience. As a result, HyperDocs were born and we were able to make a concrete shift in the student experience. Instead of writing lesson plans in a book for us as teachers to implement, we started designing lesson plans for the students using a variety of web tools, and a ripple effect of positive personalized instruction began to happen in our classrooms.

By building multiple, effective educational philosophies into each HyperDoc, each digital lesson has the potential to upend the way you instruct with technology. The reason HyperDocs work is because each one begins with a strong lesson design, curates quality instructional content, and packages learning in a way that engages learners. A HyperDoc shifts the focus from teacher-led lectures to student-driven, inquiry-based learning, allowing students to actually learn through exploration.

HyperDocs encourage collaboration, giving every student a voice and a chance to be heard by their classmates. HyperDocs ask students to create and share authentic products, helping them develop their critical thinking and problem-solving skills, which means the teacher isn't stuck in the front of the classroom explaining every step of a lesson. It also means that teachers have more time to work with small groups and personalize the learning process to fit each student's needs.

In short, HyperDocs bring innovation into classrooms and transform the student-learning experience by answering the question, "What is it I can do now that I couldn't do before?" Our hope is that this book will become a helpful guide as you incorporate HyperDocs into your instruction and discover what's possible for your students.

Before we get into the how-to of HyperDocs, let us share a little about how and why we started using them in our classrooms. Perhaps our stories will spark an *aha* moment for you. If nothing else, we hope they'll help you see how these digital lessons can transform the learning experience in your classroom.

Our HyperDoc Aha Moments

Searching for Solutions

As an instructional technology coach, I (Lisa) was thrilled when the Common Core nationwide assessment began requiring the use of technology in classrooms. But I was also concerned that the devices schools were purchasing would only be used for testing. I knew we needed to create a way for teachers to instruct effectively with technology while simultaneously accomplishing all they are required to do. Out of this need came HyperDocs.

When I initially started using HyperDocs, I saw how my students were more independent, thinking at a higher level, and actively engaging with the lesson. My role in the classroom had changed from lecturer to facilitator. Instead of walking a student through a lesson, I suddenly had time to spend with small groups and offer personalized instruction while the rest of the class continued working its way through a HyperDoc.

When I started introducing teachers to the HyperDocs method of delivering lessons, I witnessed how the ease of creation allowed the content to be the most important part of the HyperDoc. I saw teachers reintroduce the creative process into their lesson planning and exercise the craft and skill that had drawn them to teaching in the first place. The excitement teachers experienced while creating quality learning experiences for their students fueled their energy to do a job that can seem impossible at times. Seeing that shift inspired me.

HyperDocs aren't the one-size-fits-all answer to everything we need for great instruction; they do require time, energy, and thinking. But they are a concrete solution that we, as educators, have been in dire need of for a very long time—a solution that anyone can create and implement.

From PDF to Possibility

As a teacher, I (Kelly) received an email one day from my principal letting the staff know that we had an upcoming assembly. It was going to be hosted by Cheza Nami, a non-profit that promotes global citizenship through African song-and-dance demonstrations. Attached to the email was a PDF of lesson plans for before and after the experience.

When I opened the PDF, I discovered that while there were several valuable lessons, I knew I wouldn't get to them all; and like most teachers, I was concerned about how much class time the lessons would take. However, I wanted to maintain the integrity of the Cheza Nami content, so I quickly calculated how much time I would need and realized the lessons required several forty-five-minute blocks of time. Overwhelmed, I needed a solution.

At that point, I realized I could take each lesson's objectives from the PDF and package them into a single HyperDoc. The learning process shifted from teacher-directed to inquiry-based and collaborative. I even added an option for extended thinking. When I brought my students into the computer lab and they began exploring my HyperDoc, I watched as they became engaged and motivated to learn. Excitement filled the room with a delightful hum. It was then that I knew we were onto something special. I realized I could provide higher levels of understanding in less time, something that felt like a huge accomplishment to a busy teacher like me.

Cheza Nami HyperDoc

goo.gl/Scx22U

goo.gl/yR1aro

From Curriculum Consumer to Creator

As a literacy coach, I (Sarah) have learned two critical things about myself: I love designing curriculum, and I have a nagging desire to stay organized. The curriculum designer in me takes comfort in knowing where I've been in my teaching and where I'm going, while my inner designer enjoys creating visually engaging content. So when I created my first HyperDoc, a digital storytelling mini-unit, I thought through the whole unit and designed a series of lessons in a sequential, logical order, all living in just *one* HyperDoc. With just one click, I could push out an entire study unit to my class. No more stapling packets together, no more photocopies, and no more project-management issues. It was *my* HyperDoc *aha* moment!

So how did my digital storytelling mini-unit transform my students' learning experience? Students learn in a multitude of ways using different organizational systems. Some students need to have all of the content in one place, so they can go back and reference (and re-reference) prior learning, while others prefer to work ahead or have a sense of where the unit is going. Both groups can simply scroll to a section in the HyperDoc and either "preview" or "reteach themselves" as needed. By preparing an entire unit in one HyperDoc, I provided the opportunity for *all* of my students to work at their own pace, creating a class of independent learners.

Once I saw my students' success, I used Google's *Share* button to share my mini-unit with my colleagues so they could see how simple it was to get kids going on the HyperDoc. With embedded videos and directions, they could set students up for independence without a lot of time or hassle. With one digital storytelling HyperDoc, even more students beyond my classroom could begin to create digital content. I'm happy to see my love of curriculum design spread to more classrooms.

Each of us, after enjoying the experience of designing and delivering instruction for students using HyperDocs, began to share lessons with our colleagues. HyperDocs became a part of our daily routine in the classroom. This book is a guide to digital lesson design and delivery of HyperDocs. It is a handbook. So keep it close as a reference guide for ideas and implementation. We've created HyperDocs.co to accompany this book and provide you with access to the digital lessons we introduce and explain. Use the links and QR codes throughout the book to further explore these lessons. Once you find a lesson you want to try in your classroom, make a copy of the document and revise it to fit the needs of your students. You can also share original HyperDocs you create on our website at Teachers Give Teachers (teachersgiveteachers.net). It's time to explore the new change agent that is transforming classrooms around the world and learn how to design and deliver your own personal HyperDocs!

"... the world at your fingertips."

HyperDocs will transform your teaching if you do it right. If your district is like mine, it hasn't purchased textbooks in years. Also, as a social studies teacher I'm always teaching my kids to find the best sources—hopefully primary or secondary sources. I started realizing that the textbooks were about as far from a primary source as a source could be. HyperDocs give you the ability to use what you need from your texts and then **incorporate the world into your lessons**. Anything you can find on the internet or the library can be added to your HyperDoc. You write your own digital textbooks. HyperDocs are also interactive so students stay engaged and can work at their own pace. They can discover on their own. *They can create on their own. You give them a push, a little nudge, and then watch them go.*

Probably the best byproduct besides student engagement and a deeper, richer way to share curriculum with students is that they can be and, in my opinion, should be shared... with everyone. As a teacher, I am mostly begging, borrowing, and stealing, so why not share my riches? I've been inspired by teachers from across the country and by those just down the hall in my own department. The more people you can add to your PLN the more you will learn and be able to share with your students. *It's easy to get stagnant when you're in your own box but just as easy to get inspired when you have the world at your fingertips.*

Rocky Logue, @slogue89
history teacher

1
Transformative Instruction

The Digital Age allows us to expand the way we teach. A HyperDoc transforms teaching and learning. It changes the atmosphere in a way that allows us to personalize our instruction and meet all of our students' needs.

Traditionally, instruction has been teacher-directed and textbook-driven. HyperDocs, however, allow us to package lesson plans with the student in mind, to create learning experiences that highlight *how* students learn rather than simply emphasize *what* students learn, and to use the many web resources available. In short, HyperDocs engage the twenty-first-century learner.

Methods of Delivery: Pedagogy and Practice

Pedagogy is the method and practice of teaching. When creating HyperDocs, teachers first consider the pedagogy that they will use to deliver the instruction. In this section of the handbook, we share a variety of strategies to deliver instruction on a HyperDoc in a blended learning classroom.

Personalized Instruction

In each of our classrooms, we have a variety of students who learn in a variety of ways, from Gifted and Talented Education (GATE), Resource Specialist Program (RSP), and English Language Learners (ELL) students, to students with 504 plans. HyperDocs make personalized instruction possible.

In fact, the Universal Design for Learning (UDL) encourages us to design and adapt our curriculum. So with the UDL fundamentals in mind, we can design self-paced HyperDocs that promote high expectations, use flexible methods and materials, and accurately assess student progress."[1]

Flexible Grouping

When we say "flexible grouping," we're referring to the different groupings that we use in our instruction, such as whole group, partnerships or small groups, or independent application time. You can build in several flexible grouping opportunities within a HyperDoc. For example, you could initially introduce a concept to the entire class, and then students could explore and discuss the concept with a partner or in small groups before eventually applying what they learned independently.

Ways to group students in a HyperDoc:
- Whole class on one Doc ("All students, share your thinking within the table.")
- Partnerships ("Brainstorm with your partner on this doc.")
- Small groups ("With your team, create a shared map.")
- Individual ("On your own, show what you learned.")
- Global partnerships ("For the Global Read Aloud, connect with other classrooms.")

Collaboration

HyperDocs enable us to maximize our class time and eliminate the "one hand at a time" discussion. For example, by having students click one link that goes to a collaborative tool in a HyperDoc, a class discussion can attain 100 percent participation in a short time. This also allows students who may not be comfortable sharing their ideas aloud in class to have the opportunity to be heard. Face time with students can then be repurposed, changing the starting line for complex lessons.

Project-Based Learning

The investigation of a complex question, problem, or challenge is called project-based learning (PBL), and a HyperDoc can help thoughtfully organize this process, improving both collaboration and expectation setting as a result. By providing students with quality, curated resources for investigation, building background knowledge on a topic becomes a task, rather than a lecture. As a result, the HyperDoc becomes the student's home base, where he can meet up with his peers, share what he's discovered, and decide how to build the final product. As the teacher, you gain a bird's-eye view of the process and can observe and nudge the student along the way, enabling him to take responsibility for completing the unit, something that PBL strives to accomplish yet can prove difficult to manage.

---

1 "Q & A for ELL," National Center for Universal Design on Learning, Accessed September 29, 2015, udlcenter.org/sites/udlcenter.org/files/UDL_ELLfactsheets.pdf.

Inquiry Method

The inquiry method is a student-centered, hands-on, and minds-on approach to learning. It sparks a student's curiosity and encourages self-motivation, leaving you to do little or no direct instruction. Instead, students rely upon their own observations and investigative questioning to learn the content. A HyperDoc gives a place to curate information and pose a driving question to launch student learning.

Blended Learning

The ebb and flow between teacher- and student-directed learning is called "blended learning." A blended learning classroom offers students a variety of teaching strategies, uses both paper and digital tools, and is thoughtfully orchestrated to meet teaching objectives. A HyperDoc can package all of these elements in an accessible, organized manner.

Innovative Learning Spaces

In an effort to design a space that promotes a more student-centric classroom, many schools are changing the look and feel of learning spaces by trading in desks and rows for more flexible furniture that supports collaboration. This shift in classroom design will inevitably make traditional instruction impossible—we cannot simply change our learning spaces without also changing the way we teach. HyperDocs offer a solution, bridging the gap between the space in which students learn and the methods by which they learn. The HyperDoc lesson is now in the direct hands of the student, which alters the environment completely because the teacher is no longer at the front of the classroom directing the learning space.

Distance Learning

Teachers and students are often pulled out of the classroom for various reasons. When that happens, we can rely upon distance-learning methods, or delivering instruction outside the traditional classroom setting. HyperDocs can help us stay connected with students through homework, sub plans, independent study, homeschooling, and other alternative education scenarios. Distance learning allows us to answer students' questions, provide immediate feedback on work, and maintain communication.

"...helps to differentiate and meet the needs of all learners."

Venturing into this school year, I knew I wanted to *blend technology* into my room on a regular basis. HyperDocs are not only a fabulous tool to use as I teach my students new information. They are also a tool for the students to use individually. HyperDocs have allowed me to do many things.

1. They provide me an easy way to share information with my students (text, video clips, pictures), and not just one of each, but many, along with collecting their learning at the same time. I am able to build their knowledge base more fully which *helps to differentiate and meet the needs of all learners.*

2. As a teacher, HyperDocs provide a tool for me to *create units and truly intertwine my curriculum at a higher level.* In science I created a unit because we do not have curriculum. It was amazing for the students, and I loved the process. Furthermore, the work is done for next year; I will only have to adapt it.

3. HyperDocs have completely transformed my thinking as an educator. It allows me to provide instruction at a new level and *give feedback and individualized instruction* more easily.

Kathleen Whitworth
elementary teacher

Meet All Students' Needs

HyperDocs are for *all students*. After all, the student *is* at the center of the HyperDoc experience. Whether you're a general education teacher or you work with specialized groups of learners, you can adapt HyperDocs to fit your students' diverse needs.

General Education Students

Ultimately, students are the ones who will most interact with the learning embedded in a HyperDoc. In a general education classroom, students can use Google's apps and web tools to adapt the content to fit their needs and learning styles. Students can adapt font size, colors, and other features to access the content as needed. For example, students can open HyperDocs from almost any device at school or at home, as well as organize their work in one location, such as their Google Drive, and then find it using keyword searches or shared folders. With files accessible online, learning has become paperless, which means less work gets lost at the bottom of students' backpacks. Eventually, your students might even design their own HyperDocs—something we encourage!

Resource Specialist Program

When a resource student is in our general education classroom, we can tailor our HyperDocs to meet her specific needs and goals, as stated in her Individual Education Plan (IEP), by providing direct, specialized instruction.

For students to work on a HyperDoc with modifications to meet their IEP goals, include directions to utilize various Chrome extensions or web tool resources. For example:

- IEP reading modifications can include using extensions such as Read & Write for Google or Readability that read aloud to the student or clean up a website with distracting ads. On a Google Doc, students can utilize tools such as highlighting important words and defining them with the built-in dictionary.

- IEP writing modifications can include allowing students to speak their writing ideas onto a Google Doc using the voice-typing tool or to translate ideas into multiple languages. Teachers can give direct feedback to students on a document using the comments feature or Kaizena. Kaizena is an extension that records feedback and attaches it directly to the document.

- IEP modifications that include repeating directions or small-group instruction can be met by flipping lessons. Resource students can benefit from re-reading articles or re-watching videos as many times as needed if they are linked to a HyperDoc.

English Language Learners

We often have students enter our classrooms with varying levels of English competency. To help these newcomers develop their English, we rely heavily on different strategies for environment, instruction, and Specially Designed Academic Instruction in English (SDAIE). Many of these strategies suggest developing meta-cognition, building schema, providing context, modeling, collaborating with peers, incorporating graphic organizers, representing ideas in various methods, and using the adaptive power of technology.[2]

Fortunately, we can implement the SDAIE's recommended language-development strategies and make our content more accessible to these students through a well-crafted HyperDoc and Chrome extensions. For example, when students load their HyperDoc, they can take advantage of the various web tool extensions that provide accommodations for English Language Learners:

- *Google Translate* allows students to write in their native language and translate it into English, which demonstrates their overall literacy skills. Use the link here to add this extension to your Chrome extensions: goo.gl/zH0YT.

- *Select and Speak* lets students simply highlight text in a HyperDoc, and the computer says the words. This helps emerging English speakers hear a word's pronunciation in English and become familiar with new words. Use the link here to add this extension to your Chrome extensions: goo.gl/cKjDoO.

- *Duolingo* adapts sentences to the student's fluency level, remembers troubling words the .....over which the student hovers, and shows in-text translations if they're needed. Use the link here to add this extension to your Chrome extensions: goo.gl/KF0p8Z.

HyperDocs themselves are inherently helpful for developing English speakers. For example, embedded videos allow language learners to watch—and repeatedly watch—for step-by-step visual and auditory support. This repetition can be critical for a student learning English. Captioning in videos also provides additional language support. A teacher can manually input captions in YouTube Editor. In an "explore-flip-apply" learning cycle, the student can discuss the video's content at home using their native language before participating in a class discussion. HyperDocs are often full of images, so that visual really allows the language learner to match text on the page with the content in images. An important strategy for English language students is to provide oral and written directions. HyperDocs allow for this by providing short, succinct directions right on the lesson itself, so students can easily follow along and feel successful.

Gifted and Talented Education

By their very nature, HyperDocs are perfect for Gifted and Talented Education (GATE) and students identified as GATE. A HyperDoc's design develops the soft skills described as the four C's (critical thinking and problem solving, communication, collaboration, and creation and innovation), and we can customize our HyperDocs to connect with what we're teaching in our classrooms. An article published by the Davidson Institute for Talent Development, "Tips for Teachers: Successful Strategies for Teaching Gifted Learners," suggests we offer

2 "Effective Teaching Strategies for English Language Learners," SupportREALteachers.org, Accessed November 18, 2015, www.supportrealteachers.org/strategies-for-english-language-learners.html.

GATE students acceleration opportunities to deepen content understanding, which a HyperDoc's complex extension activities accomplish. Further, when we integrate HyperDocs into our lessons, PBL becomes embedded in the students' learning cycle and they gain endless opportunities to explore, explain, apply, and create. To students who become experts on a topic, we recommend giving a platform such as a student-created HyperDoc, screencast, video, tutorial, or presentation, to share what they know. This alone elevates the expertise in the classroom and gives GATE students an opportunity to practice the important soft skills they'll need to succeed in today's global society.

504 Plans

When a student is struggling but doesn't meet the criteria for special education, a 504 plan may be created to accommodate their specific learning needs. In a digital environment, we can address many of these needs by personalizing HyperDocs. Through simple adjustments to an existing HyperDoc, such as changing the font size, creating a dark background with a light-colored font to decrease eyestrain, and including visual clues and images to improve comprehension, we can greatly improve a student's ability to access our curriculum. Even creating and filling a table with instructions, links, and spaces for students to provide answers in a HyperDoc can make all the difference for students who lack focus or organization. They no longer have to face the blank page, but can instead follow visual clues and prompts to complete tasks with increased independence.

HyperDocs Are for All Educators

Many educators are involved in a student's learning experience, and a HyperDoc can connect any or all of those educators at any given time.

Teachers, TK–12

TK–12 classroom teachers can use HyperDocs for individual lessons or unit planning, setting students up for self-paced work. No longer left to stand at the front of the classroom, teachers instead log steps as they move around and provide individualized, instant feedback. This real-time conferring is what ultimately pushes students forward and helps teachers go down their list of students with whom they need to work.

Substitutes

Rather than writing plans for a substitute teacher, teachers can create a HyperDoc with a detailed lesson plan and a personalized URL that students can access. The substitute teacher then becomes a facilitator, providing support as needed; teachers can check in and monitor student progress on the HyperDoc without being physically present, and students feel empowered because their learning is left in their hands for the day.

Specialists

Those who teach specialized content areas, including science, physical education (PE), music, and computers, can integrate HyperDocs into their classrooms as well. For example, in music, students can access content through videos and engaging apps; in PE, students can watch tutorials on a YouTube playlist and then jot down their observations in a shared HyperDoc; and in science, groups in multiple classes can gather and compare data for a weather unit. The resulting HyperDocs communicate what learning looks like in a "specialized" classroom to other teachers and parents who might not otherwise know.

Special Educators

HyperDocs can help special education teachers support their resource students' needs and realize their potential by making technology easily accessible. For example, special education teachers can integrate web tools and apps, such as a text-to-speech Chrome extension or a video tutorial, into a HyperDoc and format it to fit a student's individual education plan. Teachers can then routinely make copies of that personalized HyperDoc to share with him. Students in special education often benefit from routines, and reusing a personalized HyperDoc provides that consistency. Additionally, HyperDocs help special education teachers monitor and share a student's progress, promoting effective communication between all of the parties invested in a resource student's education, including general education teachers and parents.

Instructional Coaches

Instructional coaches create mentor lessons to complement adopted curriculum materials and regularly work with teachers to promote a shared vision for the school district. Through HyperDocs, these coaches can create a learning experience that goes beyond textbooks and then push it out to all of their district's teachers at once. And if they share their HyperDocs through social media (Twitter, Google+, etc.), instructional coaches have the opportunity to collaborate with other districts as well.

Professional Developers

Just like in a classroom, when a professional developer uses HyperDocs in his instruction, effective participation and collaboration are encouraged; information is presented in visual, innovative ways; and the professional developer becomes free to move about the room and work closely with participants. Rethinking adult-learning opportunities is critical when presenting complex and often-challenging topics. It's beneficial for teachers to see the technology practices they're being encouraged to actively use in their classrooms. In short, using HyperDocs for professional development showcases effective modern-day learning strategies.

Administrators

Administrators can design engaging HyperDocs for use in staff meetings to curate links, share content, and build a sense of community. When administrators model this kind of innovative practice, they're encouraging teachers to take risks and incorporate technology into their everyday teaching. Plus, what teacher doesn't want a more engaging meeting?

Parents

HyperDocs play a vital piece in the teacher-student-parent communication puzzle. When a parent asks his child, "What did you learn in school today?" the parent will no longer have to hear the dreaded response of "nothing." Now, with one click of the *Share* button, teachers can give parents access to their child's progress and homework, using any device at any time, and students will thrive knowing their parents and teachers are on the same page (Figure 1-3).

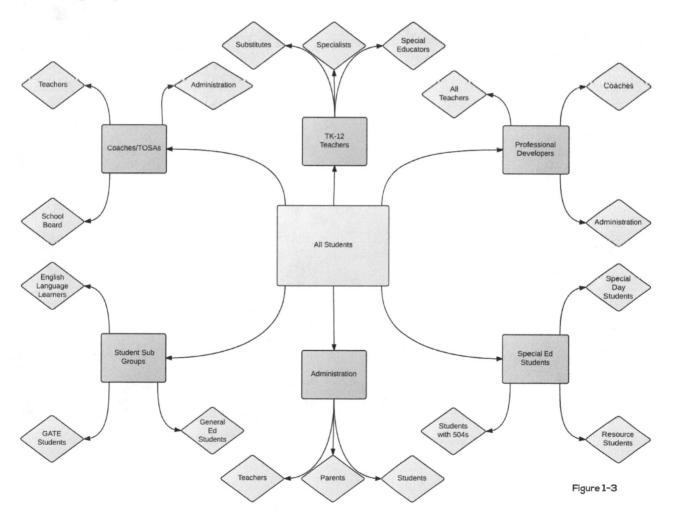

Figure 1-3

"...allowed us to move deeper within the SAMR model..."

If I had to pick my favorite current tech tool, it would be, without a doubt, the amazing HyperDoc. To say that I LOVE HyperDocs would be an extreme understatement. HyperDocs are a game changer for us at Sun Terrace Elementary. The creating and implementing of HyperDocs by almost every teacher in grades 1–5 at our site has *allowed us to move deeper within the SAMR model,* from Substitution to Modification and even Redefinition. HyperDocs give our teachers a way to clearly integrate technology tools into their instruction and, in turn, *cultivate a classroom of creators—not just consumers of information.*

Connecting with other educators on Twitter (using #HyperDocs) has given me the opportunity to not only share the HyperDocs I have made with others, but has expanded my professional learning network to include an amazing group of teachers from all across the country who have shared their creations as well. No more "reinventing the wheel" since a shared HyperDoc can be copied and revised to fit the exact needs of your students. Because of the collaborative nature of Google Tools and HyperDocs, I was able to connect with a fourth-grade teacher in Virginia (Justin Birckbichler) to create an awesome Digital Citizenship HyperDoc focusing on plagiarism and we have yet to meet in person! I feel like this is what it means to truly be a connected educator.

Karly Moura, @KarlyMoura
instructional coach

2
How to Create a HyperDoc

Even when we're delivering the "same ol' district-mandated curriculum," creating HyperDocs makes us feel alive again. We find real joy when we feel empowered as lesson designers. That's why we encourage you to draw inspiration from your students, your colleagues, and your life itself. Believe it or not, some of our best HyperDocs have come about after watching a touching video on YouTube and saying, "We need to HyperDoc that!"

Sitting down to create a HyperDoc is an opportunity to craft a meaningful, powerful experience for students. We have done our best to simplify the creation process, and while this is certainly not an exhaustive list of design tips and packaging options, it is a starting point. That's due in part to technology. Part of what makes technology so wonderful is that it is always changing, offering new tools and ideas for innovation. But at the same time, part of what makes technology so challenging is that it is always changing, insisting we constantly adapt and grow.

Technology sparks innovation, and while HyperDoc creators adapt to utilizing a variety of web tools, there are countless ways to design and create a HyperDoc. You will find yourself personalizing HyperDocs to fit your classroom, your students, and your needs. And HyperDocs aren't meant to replace your school's or district's set curriculum; rather, they should *enhance* it. Catlin Tucker, author of *Blended Learning in Grades 4–12,* notes, "Teachers must be the architects of learning." We want you to feel empowered—you're not just an assigner, you're a designer! Create. Transform. Enjoy.

Create a HyperDoc in Five Steps

1. Determine your objectives.
2. Select which learning cycle you will use.
3. Select your packaging.
4. Build the workflow.
5. Design your HyperDoc.

Step 1: Determine Your Objectives

As educators, we are content designers. Day in and day out, we ask ourselves, "What is my content? And how will I *deliver* the content?" These are fundamental questions in a teacher's daily life. Whatever jargon we use to express our lessons' learning objectives, there are some universal core elements we should consider when designing HyperDocs.

Grade Level—A HyperDoc can be adapted up or down to meet students' needs, grade-level-specific content needs, and state standards—meaning students of all ages and all grade levels can benefit from the engagement strategies embedded within the document. For primary learners, in transitional kindergarten through second grade, a HyperDoc becomes a launch pad for the day's lesson. A primary school teacher might work off of one HyperDoc and do more demonstration strategies with his students, whereas students in second and third grade are becoming more and more independent, so a teacher can ask them to log in and access information using Google Apps for Education. And students in fourth through twelfth grades are absolutely capable of accessing a HyperDoc and independently working through the digital lesson plan.

Content Area—Elementary school teachers are expected to create and implement lesson plans for multiple subjects, including reading, writing, math, science, social studies, character education, and art. To fit all of these subjects within a given day or time period, teachers prepare cross-curricular lessons and projects. HyperDocs are the perfect solution for the elementary school teacher who wants to either focus on a single subject area or combine multiple disciplines into one digital experience.

Secondary school teachers are masters of their content, and they work to develop innovative ways to deliver their particular subject area's content. Lessons are typically part of a larger study unit, and they may be individual or repeated throughout the day in different periods and classes. HyperDocs allow the teacher to curate specific content and individual lessons over a course of study. Teachers could even promote collaborative conversations across their classrooms on a given topic. For example, by eighth period, multiple classes would have communicated in one HyperDoc.

Length of Lesson—One HyperDoc might be given as a pre-unit exploration where students revisit the HyperDoc over the course of a week, while another HyperDoc might span an entire unit of study for a few weeks. When creating a HyperDoc, ask yourself, "How long will my class use this?"

Specific Objective—As you begin to think about your HyperDoc, establish clear objectives. You may have a simple, singular teaching point or purpose in mind or an overarching set of essential questions that serve a more comprehensive outcome. You could take a direct approach in your HyperDoc and clearly state the purpose at the top for students to see, or you could be more subtle in the delivery of your learning objectives. Whatever you choose, as you set out to design your digital lesson plans, consider the vision you have for your learning objectives.

Desired Outcome—When you begin designing your HyperDoc, think about what your desired outcome for the learner will be. This could include:

- *Exploring* a concept or topic in depth or simply piquing interest
- *Discussing* collaboratively online
- *Creating* something from scratch to engage learners
- *Applying* knowledge to extend a concept
- *Assessing* student learning

Step 2: Select Which Learning Cycle You Will Use

New and veteran teachers alike will agree that lesson design is a complex, personal process. Every single lesson plan and unit of study we create requires both formal and technical components. As time progresses and we become more experienced, lesson design begins to feel more personal, and yet very technical. As we craft lessons, we should be considering the following questions:

- How do I craft an *essential question*?
- What does an *anticipatory set* involve?
- How can I immediately engage students with a powerful *hook*?
- Is there a set amount of time for *reflection*?
- What artifact will students create to show that my teaching has stuck?

HyperDocs can address these questions as well as many others in the design stage.

Popular Learning Cycles—Some learning cycles have stood the test of time, while others are more progressive, more recent models. Some of the more prevalent learning cycles in today's classrooms include:

- Explore-Explain-Apply or Explore-Flip-Apply

- Workshop Model: Connect, Teach, Engage, Application, Reflection

- 5E Instructional Model: Engage, Explore, Explain, Elaborate, Evaluate[3]

- HyperDoc Model: Engage, Explore, Explain, Apply, Share, Reflect, Extend

Many of our HyperDocs are a hybrid of these learning cycles, with each lesson's purpose deciding which learning cycles are used. We recommend that you first determine which of these learning cycles (or your own) is best suited for your HyperDoc before getting started so that you can provide a structure for your lesson design. Like us, you probably teach with intention and purpose, so you'll find yourself using different cycles of learning for different reasons in your classroom. We encourage you to take liberties to create and personalize your HyperDocs to fit your individual needs.

Step 3: Select Your Packaging

While the HyperDocs concept may initially seem complicated, a HyperDoc is really just smart packaging. Think about it: What draws your attention to and piques your curiosity in a new task? What would make your students curious about learning in a new, unexpected way? Could you share that in a Google Doc?

HyperDocs move away from large blocks of text on a standard piece of white paper to an online document that is succinct, easy to comprehend independently, and engaging. Start by reimagining a course syllabus or project. Instead of giving your students a paper handout or packet, package the content in a way that makes them excited about their tasks.

Thinking about lesson design and packaging is critical. Will your HyperDoc be a view-only document that you share through a link? Do you want students to complete a form or watch a video? Do you want them to click away from the initial document, opening new tabs to access other parts of the assignment? There is no one right answer, but that's the beauty of a HyperDoc—it's unique and can reflect the needs of your lesson and the students accessing it. You may choose to create a HyperDoc using one tool, only to switch to another as you realize the new tool would better support the group you're working with.

As you create your HyperDoc, take time to process what you want your students to gain from it, and try to stay open to the idea that even once you've created it, nothing is permanent—you can always make changes.

That, in and of itself, is an important step in the design process.

---

3 "Inquiry, the Learning Cycle, & the 5E Instructional Model," Kansas Association for Conservation & Environmental Education, Accessed October 4, 2015, kacee.org/files/Inquiry & 5E Instructional Model.pdf.

How you choose to package your lesson may play a big role in its effectiveness. Consider the following options when creating your HyperDoc:

Google Docs

Using Google Docs has always been like creating a fast and simple web page. It is our go-to choice for creating a HyperDoc for so many reasons:

- Accessible from any device

- Simple to edit and revise

- Can serve as a launch pad for incredible learning experiences

- Offers numerous font choices that can help clearly identify tasks

- Enables you to embed images so that visual learners can better comprehend the content

- Allows you to adjust the background colors to reduce the glare of the white page for sensitive eyes

- Helps you organize your content and expectations using visible tables

- Permits you to hide links behind words like "here," decluttering an assignment and leading learners to external locations where the lesson continues (see Figure 2-1).

Activity 2 Theme	HyperDoc	Thinking/wonders/ideas
What defines a place?	#PlaceProject HyperMap*	Explore and think about the many examples on the Google map that help define what a place is all about. Record your thinking HERE

Figure 2-1

While Google Docs offers a quick, convenient way to create a HyperDoc, keep its limitations in mind as well. For example, aside from images, you can only *link* to videos, Google Forms, Google Presentations, and outside web tools—not embed them—requiring the viewer (student) to go to a new location to access the content. Another aspect to consider is how you will assess your students' work: Will they record their answers on the doc, or do you have to go to different web tools to check for completion of the task? There are many ways to work around these issues such as using Google Classroom, which allows you to easily view student work in one location as it is completed.

Google Slides

Many educators use Google Slides as a web tool for presenting reports and speeches. However, when we ask our students what they would do with Slides, they saw the slides as a deck of cards, a collection of "papers"—almost like a packet—that allows them to visualize the flow of an assignment as it goes from one slide to the next. Their perspective allowed us to see Google Slides in a whole new light.

When you're packaging content using Slides, keep these features in mind:

- You can embed videos on a slide, keeping your students away from YouTube and the distraction of the related videos that come up.

- You can add graphic features, such as arrows, call-out graphics, and shapes, to your slides that will add to the design of your lesson.

- You can even change the page size, creating a completely different-looking slide deck with 8.5" by 11" pages.

- Google Slides offers some of the same features as Google Docs, including fonts, colors, tables and embedded links, as well as an engaged workflow, which can be achieved depending upon how you package your instructions and tasks (see Figure 2-2).

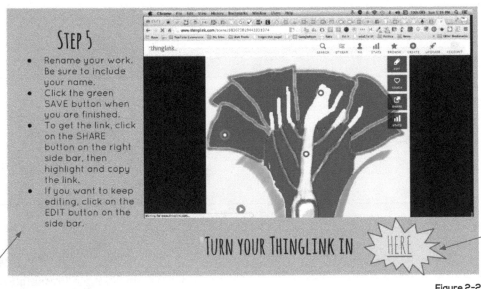

Figure 2-2

Sometimes a lesson will require collaborating directly on the slides. In this case, students can take a view-only slide deck, make a copy of it, and then add collaborators who will complete tasks on their assigned slides. Working on their own slide versus together in a Google Doc helps students learn "digital citizenship," or keeping to your own work and not deleting others', something that can be an issue if not monitored. In fact, we've often resorted to viewing a document's revision history or even changing students' share settings to emphasize the need for respecting others' digital work.

While Google Slides can help you package content in ways you may have never imagined, you will also need to consider how you'll assess your students' work. Do you want to go through each slide, one by one, or have a single slide with all of the written work in one place? Alternatively, you could add an "answer slide" that students move to the first position, giving you a very visual clue in your Drive's grid view as to when a task has been completed (see Figure 2-3). What's more, you could add a link to a Google Form, where all of your students' written responses are collected in one spreadsheet. Remember, you have options when creating an evaluation process, so experiment, make adjustments, and find one that works for both you and your students.

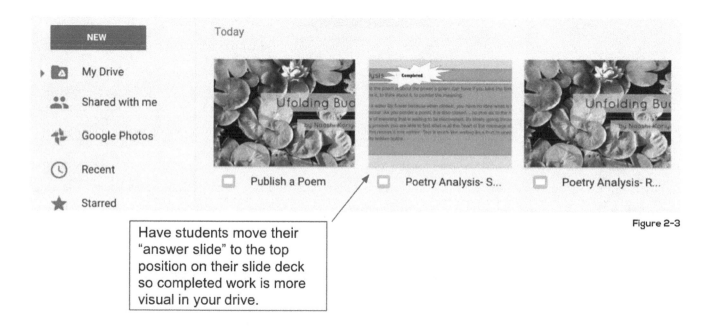

Have students move their "answer slide" to the top position on their slide deck so completed work is more visual in your drive.

Figure 2-3

Google Forms

Google Forms is a great tool to use if you're packaging videos in a lesson because it keeps students from having to link away from an assignment to view content. You can strategically post questions throughout the form according to the kind of information you want to gather from students as they progress through the lesson (see Figure 2-4).

A form's content can be broken into multiple pages and even lead a student down a specific path ("branch logic"). Remember the *Choose Your Own Adventure* books from your youth? With some planning, Google Forms can do much the same, in that, depending on how a student answers a question, the form can open to a specific follow-up question.

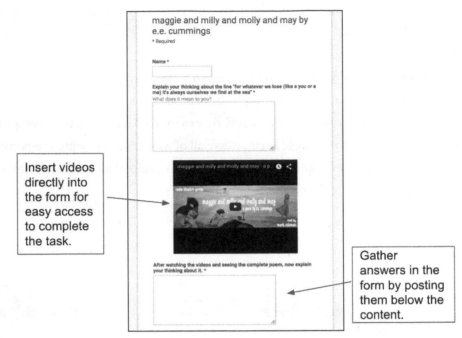

maggie and milly and molly and may by e.e. cummings
* Required

Name *

Explain your thinking about the line "for whatever we lose (like a you or a me) it's always ourselves we find at the sea" *
What does it mean to you?

After watching the videos and seeing the complete poem, now explain your thinking about it. *

Insert videos directly into the form for easy access to complete the task.

Gather answers in the form by posting them below the content.

Figure 2-4

When we want to create a HyperDoc to collect individual student feedback for fast, efficient evaluation, we use a Google Form. In a single form, post instructions, images, and videos alongside questions that students can "turn in," all in one location. Students' answers are then collected in one place in a spreadsheet, allowing the teacher to see all of their responses at one time, which can be a big time-saver if you teach multiple classes. Google Forms is great for multiple-choice questions, short answers, gathering feedback, and short paragraphs.

Although students can't directly collaborate using Google Forms, you can link a response spreadsheet to a HyperDoc when you want your students to share their answers with one another. This has been a game changer in our classrooms. The time we had previously dedicated to each student individually sharing ideas and projects can now be maximized, with students now exploring their classmates' work instantly and independently through a link (see Figure 2-5).

Student responses can be shared by providing a link to the spreadsheet

	A	B	C	D	E	F	G
1	Timestamp	Name	Explain your thinking about the line "for whatever we lose (like a you or a me) it's always ourselves we find at the sea"	After watching the videos and seeing the complete poem, now explain your thinking about it.	How did your thinking change?	How did seeing the three different versions of the poem affect your thinking about it?	Comments
16	5/20/2013 19:16:57	Brent	If you lose your purpose, you can be lost in a sea of people who will never know what you could have been.	I think now that it means that you can find anything that you love at the ocean.	It changed my perspective on the ocean.	It didn't really change my thinking except for the first one that showed the whole poem.	This is a really cool poem!
17	5/20/2013 19:21:37	Ryan	I think it means that when you lose someone you love it gets really emotional and start crying creating the sea.	The sea contains happy memories and when you're sad you go to somewhere where good memories live. That can lift your spirits up.	Well, at first I was all this isn't complete and then you showed us the video and a light bulb went off.	Well the third one didn't change anything about my thinking because it was sooooooooooo weird!!! I liked the second one best because the picture went along with the words and the song.	

Figure 2-5

Google Sites

When you're packaging a large unit or project, or if you simply want all of your lesson's components embedded in one location, consider building a website using Google Sites. This can be a great choice because your students never have to link away from the HyperDoc's initial set of instructions.

Google Sites features include the following options:

- Create a visual flow to a project, allowing students to progress at their own rate.

- Simply organize resources since you can post multiple documents in a logical manner.

- Include Google Forms for students to turn in a completed project link using embedding features.

- Visually post published student work on a class "digital bulletin board" with embedded projects posted for easy viewing and sharing (see Figure 2-6).

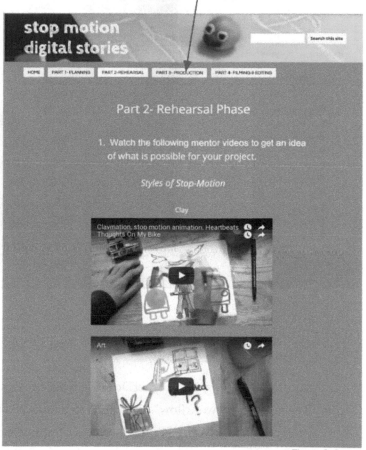

Build a lesson on a Google Site with easy to follow instructions and resources.

Figure 2-6

Google My Maps

Everything happens somewhere, so why not place the content you're sharing with your students on a map? The idea of using My Maps to create HyperDocs came from Jo-Ann Fox, a teacher in San Diego, California. Using My Maps, you can place location markers anywhere in the world. And once a marker is set, you can add images, videos, text, and even links to it. What's more, not only can students explore a marker's content, they can also explore the area around a marker by zooming in on the map.

My Maps is also collaborative and enables students to become content creators. Each student can place markers full of information that anyone with a link to the map can immediately access and explore.

As you continue to explore creative packaging ideas for your HyperDocs, think about the web tools you could use. Package content using anything that helps you organize; has text, image, and video capabilities; and can link to external sites if needed (see Figure 2-7).

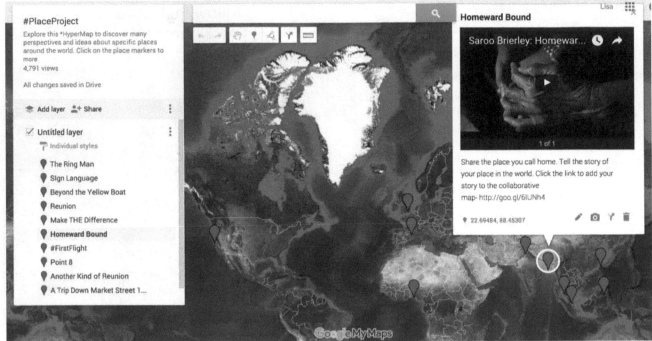

Figure 2-7

Step 4: Build the Workflow

As you start designing your HyperDoc, you'll need to determine how you will take your work from initiation to completion, or your "workflow," and which web tools will prove most efficient.

In our experience creating HyperDocs, we've found Google Apps offer layers of workflow options because all of Google's applications are collaborative and can be published on the Internet. If you're new to Google Apps, designing a HyperDoc and its workflow may take some practice; but as you create more HyperDocs, you will become more proficient in reimagining ways to use your web tools.

As you make decisions and select your web tools, consider these four questions:

Share: How will I push out or share my HyperDoc with students?

Feedback: How will I interact with students and provide feedback?

Collection: How will I collect my students' thoughts, work, or products?

Clicks: How many clicks will it take to view a student's work?

In this section, we will address the workflow from a HyperDoc that begins on your Google Drive and a HyperDoc that begins in your Google Classroom.

From the Google Drive

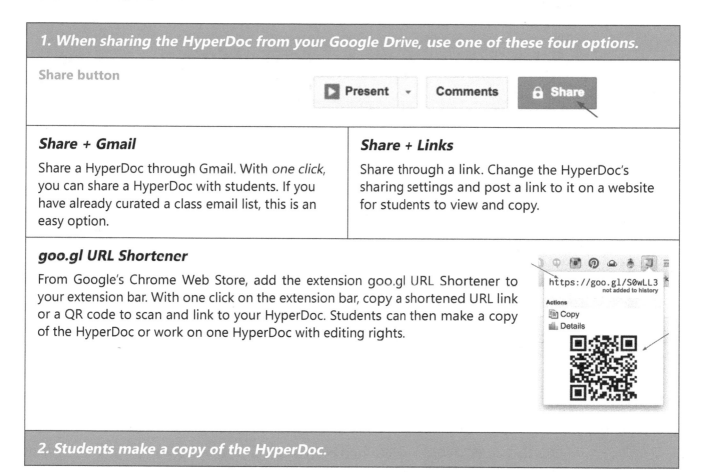

1. When sharing the HyperDoc from your Google Drive, use one of these four options.

Share button

Share + Gmail	**Share + Links**
Share a HyperDoc through Gmail. With *one click*, you can share a HyperDoc with students. If you have already curated a class email list, this is an easy option.	Share through a link. Change the HyperDoc's sharing settings and post a link to it on a website for students to view and copy.

goo.gl URL Shortener

From Google's Chrome Web Store, add the extension goo.gl URL Shortener to your extension bar. With one click on the extension bar, copy a shortened URL link or a QR code to scan and link to your HyperDoc. Students can then make a copy of the HyperDoc or work on one HyperDoc with editing rights.

2. Students make a copy of the HyperDoc.

3. Use comments for feedback.

Comment on student work and provide feedback while students are working on the HyperDoc. Don't wait until the final assignment is turned in.

4. Collect student work using one of these four options.

New Folders

1. Create a new folder on your Google Drive and place your HyperDoc in it.

2. Share your folder with students.

3. Students make a copy of the original HyperDoc and complete the tasks.

4. Students move their own version of the HyperDoc into the shared folder.

5. From the shared folder, click each student's HyperDoc and use the comment features to interact and provide feedback.

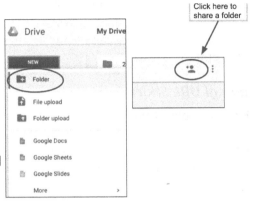

Shared with Me

1. Students will share work with the teacher using the share settings on a document.
2. HyperDocs can be found in the "Shared with Me" section of your Drive.
3. Interact with students using the comment features on the document.
4. Organize student HyperDocs in your Drive using folders.

Google Forms

1. From the original HyperDoc, attach a link to a Google Form. In the form, students attach the link to their completed HyperDoc.
2. View all student work from a Google Sheets spread sheet attached to the form.

Google Docs with Sheets or Slides

1. Open the share settings on the Doc, Sheets, or Slides and choose "anyone with a link can edit."
2. Share the link to the Doc, Sheets, or Slides using Gmail or a shortened URL.
3. Invite students to add their work in a Sheet or on a Slide to link completed projects.
4. Talk about digital citizenship and honoring the work that each person does on the Doc or Slide.

From Google Classroom

If a HyperDoc begins in your Google Classroom, follow these workflow steps:

1. Share from Google Classroom

1. Add an assignment.
2. Attach a HyperDoc.
3. Choose a workflow option:
   - Students can view the file.
   - Students can edit the file.
   - Make a copy for each student.

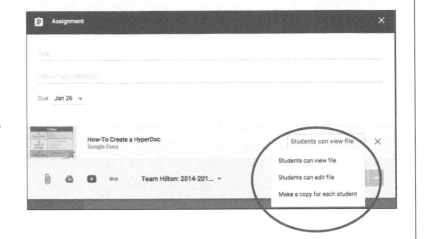

2. Feedback and Collection

Use comments for feedback or send feedback through Google Classroom. Collect all of your students' work in the virtual classroom.

1. Add an assignment.
2. Choose the "add a question" feature.
3. Students respond to the question by posting a link to their completed work.
4. You can quickly view who turned in the assignment and send feedback to students. (This option for collection involves fewer clicks.)
5. Students can interact and comment on one another's work like a social media conversation thread.

If you are interested in learning more about how to use Google Classroom, we recommend reading *50 Things You Can Do with Google Classroom* by Alice Keeler and Libbi Miller.

Step 5: Design Your HyperDoc

In learning, as in life, aesthetics matter. A HyperDoc can instantly engage and entice learners through its use of colors, layout, images, videos, and text arrangement. Additionally, we can appeal to the learning needs of the many students who identify as visual learners through well-designed HyperDocs.

As you create your HyperDocs and make design choices, keep your students in mind. We'll walk through some of the steps needed to create a digital lesson plan targeting your learners' needs—whether you teach kindergarteners who require simple directions with bright colors, middle schoolers who want a one-pager with step-by-step directions, high schoolers who can follow a more independent "choose your own adventure" lesson, or even adult learners who are comfortable exploring articles and videos on a complex topic.

When designing a HyperDoc, consider:

- The age of your learners

- How many clicks will be required

- Font size and readability

- Balance of text and images

- If there is a theme with which to work

- If you'll use a color scheme to make the content more memorable

- The lesson's flow (Will it be a one-pager or study unit?)

Page Color and Size Layout

Page color and size layout are among the first, and easiest, ways to entice learners. For example, if you're developing a lesson set in the silent film era, you could choose a black background with white font to replicate a black-and-white film. The page size you choose for your layout will also set a tone for your HyperDoc. If you want to use large photos and large letters for primary students, you may opt for a land-scape layout (Figure 2-8).

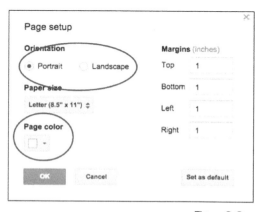

Figure 2-8

Images

Today's learners must quickly read and interpret visual images on a regular basis. These are the visual literacy skills that we can help learners cultivate by creating lesson plans that include engaging images to instantly capture their attention and set a tone for learning. As you design your HyperDoc, you'll decide not only the types of images you want to incorporate into your lesson but, more importantly, the *tone* you want to set with the images. Is this a history lesson, making primary sources the best choice? Or is the lesson a personal narrative and you want to personalize the content using photos of yourself? Some of your options include:

- Your own photos or photos from Creative Commons licenses

- Clip art

- Animated GIFs

- Designs you've created in Google Drawings

How to insert an image (Figure 2-9)

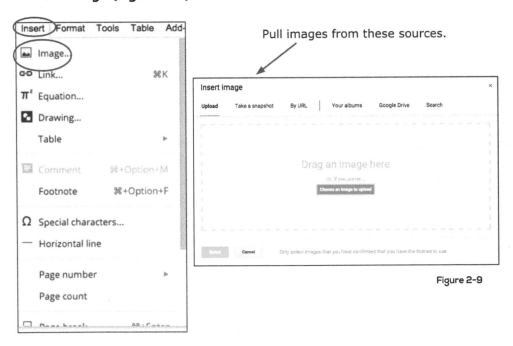

Figure 2-9

We support teachers and students using images that have been labeled for reuse (see Figure 2-10).

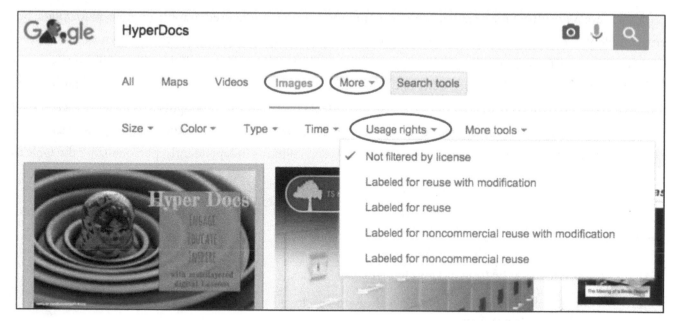

Figure 2-10

Links

Part of what makes HyperDocs so teacher friendly is that you, as the teacher, can customize directions and insert links specific to a lesson. Students are not left to search the Internet on their own, but instead are able to explore your handpicked content.

Videos

It's a fact: Twenty-first-century students are surrounded by video, and they read and interpret meaning from video just as they would from a printed text. This combination of auditory and visual cues maximizes the brain's ability to understand the meaning of the video. In the classroom, students can travel anywhere through videos; they can see and hear people around the world, experience science in a visual way, and take in stimuli that reach parts of the brain that a page in a textbook simply can't.

If you're using a Google Doc, you cannot embed a video on the page, so you'll need to insert a link to the video. Follow these steps:

1. Go to the video and copy the link.

2. Type the title of the video in the Google Doc.

3. Highlight the title, go to *Insert*, and then click *Link* (see Figure 2-11).

4. Paste the video link into the field provided and click *Apply*.

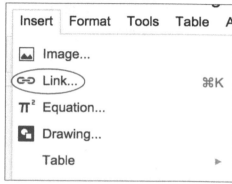

Figure 2-11

Tables

Tables are a great tool for organizing information for learners. We've used graphic organizers for years, but with a table you can simply create one in a HyperDoc and leave space for students to jot down their thinking. The more you use Table Properties, the more creative your HyperDoc's design will become. You can customize Tables in various ways with colored cells and borderline features. In an instant (and without having to make photocopies), you've just created an opportunity for students to record their thoughts and develop their digital literacy skills. As an added bonus, a student-completed table allows you to track a student's progress or can serve as an assessment. Even better, students learn to add rows and columns independently, personalizing the table to fit their own note-taking needs.

Creating a Table

1. Select *Table* from the toolbar (Figure 2-12).

2. Select the table size you need (you can always go back and add or delete a row or column).

3. Add your content.

Figure 2-12

Customizing a Table

1. Adjust the width of each cell by dragging the rule left or right.

2. Change the table border's color and width by selecting Table Properties (Figure 2-13).

3. Choose the cell background color by selecting Table Properties and picking the color you want.

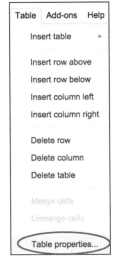
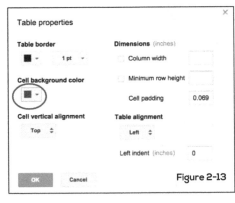

Figure 2-13

Fonts (choice, size, variety)

As insignificant as they may seem, the fonts we use actually affect a doc's tone, readability, and message. HyperDocs are a blank canvas with a wide range of font choices, so choose carefully. For example, look at any billboard, grocery store product, or magazine advertisement. Fonts brand an idea, and consistency is comfortable to the consumer. Your students are the consumers, so keep this in mind when you are designing a series of HyperDocs. Legibility depends on a combination of factors, including typeface, type size, color, line length, and spacing. Choose a font with creative style for titles and headers. Choose a simple and clean font for lengthy text (Figure 2-14).

Aside from font choice and size, consider variety. We encourage you to use interesting fonts, but keep in mind that the fonts you choose should enhance your HyperDoc, not confuse the learner. Typically, we limit our documents to only two fonts: one for headers and titles and another for text. When choosing the font you'll use for your text, opt for one that is both clear and readable because it will affect how your students' eyes are drawn to the content. Now that you have learned how to create a HyperDoc, you are ready to consider how to improve it with a "hack."

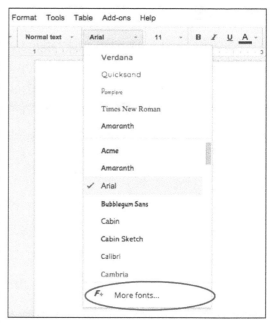

Figure 2-14

How Can You Hack a HyperDoc?

When we say "hacking," we mean a clever readjustment, breakthrough, or revision. A hack develops from a desire to want to do something better. We encourage our students to reflect so they can grow their ideas and knowledge. Just as we do with our students, we encourage you to pause and reflect on your experience, once you're creating HyperDocs on your own, so you can grow in your thinking and become a more innovative educator.

When reflecting on a HyperDoc's effectiveness, you can use well-known guidelines such as Webb's Depth of Knowledge (DOK); the Substitution, Augmentation, Modification, or Redefinition (SAMR) model; or the International Society for Technology in Education's (ISTE) standards. And since HyperDocs are digital lesson plans designed to transform the student learning experience, we use these tools to guide our lesson design and implementation just as every reflective teacher does.

Webb's DOK

Webb's DOK chart describes the performance levels where students demonstrate varying degrees of knowledge. In a HyperDoc, students shift through activities that vary their range of thinking among four levels: 1) Recall, 2) Skill/Concept, 3) Strategic Thinking, and 4) Extended Thinking. Ultimately, a HyperDoc is a conduit teachers can use to design lessons that take students through all of the levels, including Extended Thinking, by providing students the opportunity to design, create, and analyze.

Examples of DOK 4 and Extended Thinking

- *Conduct* a project that requires specifying a problem, designing and conducting an experiment, analyzing its data, and reporting your results and solutions.

- *Apply* a mathematical model to illuminate a problem or situation.

- *Analyze and synthesize* information from multiple sources.

- *Describe and illustrate* how common themes are found across texts from different cultures.

- *Design* a mathematical model to inform and solve a practical or abstract situation.

SAMR

The SAMR model, designed by Ruben Puentedura, PhD, describes technology integration through four levels defined as follows (Figure 2-15).

Substitution: Technology is used as a direct substitute for what you might do already, with no functional change.

Augmentation: Technology is a direct substitute, but there is functional improvement over what you did without the technology.

Modification: Technology allows you to significantly redesign the task.

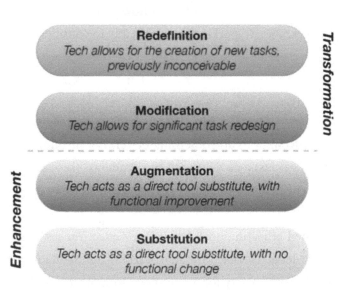

Figure 2-15

Redefinition: Technology allows you to do what was previously not possible.

Because HyperDocs have the potential to transform learning, we should ask ourselves when designing them, "Does this HyperDoc allow us to do something we couldn't do before using technology?" (See Figure 2-16.)

Mentor HyperDocs

T R A N S F O R M A T I O N

REDEFINITION
Lessons allow for creation of new tasks previously inconceivable.
e Students have an opportunity to create, collaborate, and connect beyond the classroom.

Collection of HyperDocs to teach digital skills HERE *(search, digital voice, video, digital citizenship, visual literacy)*

Curate literacy content over time on a global reading log HERE

Assessment enhanced with various "Show What You Know" tools HERE or "Choose Your Own Adventure" tools HERE

Multi-Layered Unit Planning HERE and HERE

Student-driven passion projects (20% Time/Genius Hour) HERE

Interact with students, parents, teachers with reflection HERE and HERE

Professional Development in which the teachers experience tech tools as a student HERE

MODIFICATION
Lessons allow for significant task redesign.
Students use technology to learn how to learn.

Collection of HyperDocs to extend a class read aloud HERE

Start a movement on campus with one inspiring video HERE

Reflect or revise with students and/or teacher HERE

Enhance a science article by adding in opportunities to create a digital artifact HERE

Travel the world through a storytelling map HERE

Interact with science from this digital learning slide deck HERE

Collaborative speaking and listening HERE and HERE

AUGMENTATION
Lesson plan uses tech as a direct tool substitute with functional change.
Lesson is scaffolded to build up to a transformative lesson.

Digital literacy – read text and record thinking HERE and HERE

Learn more about a topic HERE

Digitize your reading assessment by adding responses HERE

Share books and collaborate on ideas with a simple table on a HyperDoc HERE or on a slide deck HERE

Learn how to use a new web tool HERE and HERE

SUBSTITUTION
Lesson design acts as a direct tool substitute with no functional change.
Lesson is teaching foundational skills that will lead to more complex skills.

Digital note-taking and graphic organizers HERE

Create a drawing using Google Draw with figurative language HERE

Step-by-step assignment directions (watch video and draft a letter) HERE

Read and annotate digital text HERE

Community-building activity used for a Professional Development session (directions and list of activities) HERE

E N H A N C E M E N T

Figure 2-16

Scan the QR code or visit the link to see examples of HyperDocs that fit into each level of the SAMR model.

goo.gl/EkR54l

ISTE (International Society for Technology in Education)

The ISTE has designed standards for students, teachers, and coaches. After closely looking at what ISTE is asking of educators, we've concluded HyperDocs are the perfect vehicle to meet the organization's rigorous standards.

Creating and teaching with a HyperDoc requires you to plan and facilitate an experience for students that allows them to explore, explain, and apply what they discover. In this scenario, students learn *how* to learn and how to interact digitally, both locally and globally. When you take a look at the ISTE standards for teachers, you'll see how HyperDocs closely meet the expectations of all five standards. Teachers who design and deliver instruction on a HyperDoc are meeting the expectations for the ISTE standards by facilitating student learning, inspiring creativity, designing and delivering digital age learning experiences or assessments, modeling digital-age work and digital citizenship, and engaging in professional growth as new tools and technologies evolve.

ISTE Standards for Teachers

- Facilitate and inspire student learning and creativity
- Design and develop digital age learning experiences and assessments
- Model digital age work and learning
- Promote and model digital citizenship and responsibility
- Engage in professional growth and leadership

HyperDocs can always be updated to link to the most current events, resources, and information available, ensuring that what students are learning is relevant to real life. Creating HyperDocs requires educators to preview, review, and leverage online resources regularly and effectively to model and teach students technology integration. This means that teachers are consistently searching, researching, publishing, and creating skills in a digital world. To evaluate a HyperDoc and see if it meets the teacher standards, as outlined by ISTE, look at the Teacher ISTE Checklist at goo.gl/Z5tKrn.

ISTE Standards for Students

- Creativity and innovation
- Critical thinking, problem solving, and decision making
- Communication and collaboration
- Digital citizenship
- Research and information fluency
- Technology operations and concepts

As you can see, a student's experience using a HyperDoc also meets the ISTE's student standards. To evaluate a HyperDoc and see if it meets your students' needs, as outlined by ISTE, look at the Student ISTE Checklist at goo.gl/Z5tKrn.

ISTE Standards for Coaches

- Visionary leadership

- Teaching, learning, and assessments

- Digital-age learning environments

- Professional development and program evaluation

- Digital citizenship

- Content knowledge and professional growth

Instructional coaches also meet the ISTE's standards for coaches and support the movement for transforming educational practices in classrooms. For the ISTE's detailed checklist for coaches, look at the Coach ISTE Checklist at goo.gl/Z5tKrn.

The Four Cs of Transformation

While hacking your HyperDoc may initially seem complicated, you can simplify the process by thinking about how you'll provide your students with opportunities to collaborate, create, and connect while thinking critically. Ask yourself, "Have I included opportunities for my students to apply the four Cs in the HyperDoc lesson I've created? Is there an authentic way to revise my lesson to elevate its learning potential?"

As you critique your HyperDocs to ensure they're transformational learning experiences for your students, consider the following:

Create

A HyperDoc that asks students to create will engage their thinking and give you a better glimpse into their learning process. When students create, they are first required to process and synthesize, then present their interpretation of the information. Let students show you they understand the content in a HyperDoc by becoming digital directors (using movie-making tools), developers (using web tools to develop products), and designers (designing images and graphics).

Over the course of the school year, you may also consider letting your students explain and visualize their thinking, as well as show you what they've learned (a comprehensive assessment) by using creation web tools. There are so many, and they each have specific applications. Fortunately, you don't have to be proficient in using all of them. Rather, as the facilitator of learning, trust your students and use these options when asking your students to create:

1. Teacher Directed: You select the tool, teach the class how to use that tool, and then make it the only option students have for creating in the HyperDoc (See Figure 2-17).

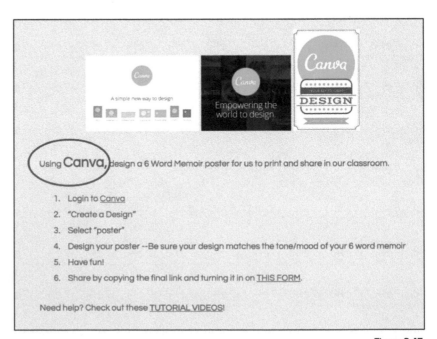

Figure 2-17

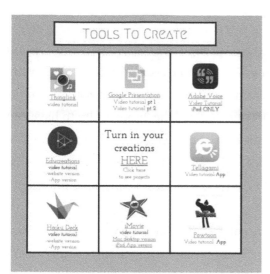

Figure 2-18

2.Student Options: Allow students to choose a creation tool from a list of options (Figure 2-18). They may use video tutorials to learn how to use the tools they choose. Also, recognize and name students who are experts at using the tools and encourage them to teach *others* how to use their tools.

goo.gl/4wpPQk

3.Choice: Give students the option of choosing their web tools. To give them ideas of which ones they could use, make a list of your favorites or create a list as a class. We've provided three sets of tools for directors, developers, and designers, which you may want to provide to students (with links) so they can determine the tools that will best fit their devices and desired outcomes (Figure 2-19).

goo.gl/qw1vmM

~ Digital Directors ~

PROGRAM	LINK	APPLICATION	DEVICE
	Powtoons	Create animated movies and insert voiceovers.	iPad, Chromebook, Mac, Web
	Educreations	Class Code: VHKMYFR Interactive white board and voice recording to teach a lesson.	iPad, Chromebook, Mac, Web
	Adobe Voice	Audio and visual story teller	iPad App
	Silent Film Studio	Create short films that have the effects of a silent film.	iPad App
	iMovie	Create video. Can also import most clips from some of these other applications.	iPad, Mac
	Tellagami	30 sec of an animated character, insert voice and background images~	iPad App
	Morfo	60 seconds of voice recording over a photo	iPad App
	WeVideo	Create shared videos online.	Chromebook, Mac, Web
	Animoto	1. Movie templates that use photos and video 2. Class Promo Code: ehehitcob360	Chromebook, Mac, Web

~ Digital Developers ~

PROGRAM	LINK	APPLICATION	DEVICE
thinglink.	Thinglink	Create resources in one place, video, text, images, etc.	iPad, Chromebook, Mac, Web
K!	Kahoot	Create online quizzes by creating your own questions.	iPad, Chromebook, Mac, Web
	Aurasma	CLICK HERE for demo. Augmented images and video information. Voiceovers to explain information.	iPad App
HAIKU DECK	Haiku Deck	Slideshow with images, graphs, charts, math	iPad, Chromebook, Mac, Web
	Google Presentation/Docs	Link resources to a presentation doc in Google Drive.	iPad, Chromebook, Mac, Web
k	Klikaklu	Klikaklu is a photo hunt game that uses your phone's GPS, camera and advanced image matching technology. It's a great way to quickly create and play treasure hunts!	iPad
	Google Sites	Design a website	iPad, Chromebook, Mac, Web

~ Digital Designers ~

PROGRAM	LINK	APPLICATION	DEVICE
floors	Floors Press Floor Lesson Plans	Draw and design your own video games.	1. Print paper from web 2. View on iPad App
	colAR Mix	Color in a coloring page. Scan it with the iPad app and the images become 3D	1. Print paper from web 2. View on iPad App
	Garageband	Create music	iPad, Mac
	Pic Collage Resources	Use photos, stickers, frames, and text to create collages.	iPad App
	Skitch	Annotate Text ~Show Places on a Map~Label Diagram	iPad App
	WordFoto	Turn Your Photos and Words into Stunning Works of Art	iPad App
	Google Draw	Draw in your Google Drive	iPad, Chromebook, Mac
	Threadsort	Send Art ~ Download to digital portfolio	iPad, Chromebook, Mac
	Scratch	Block coding program	iPad, Chromebook, Mac

Figure 2-19

Collaborate

Lev Vygotsky, a learning theorist and psychologist, said, "We learn through our interactions and communications with others."[4] ISTE's standards for teachers call upon educators to develop highly collaborative citizens, people capable of listening, paraphrasing, crafting questions, and negotiating answers. When you package the latest collaboration tools in a HyperDoc, you give all of your students the opportunity to have conversations, listen, respond appropriately, discuss topics, build on ideas or comments, ask questions, and work together toward a shared goal. Of course, there will be times when it's important to practice face-to-face communication, but balancing that interaction with digital collaboration allows everyone's voice to be heard, beyond just those raising their hands.

The following text set features some of our favorite ways to include collaboration in HyperDocs. Read through it and choose the best tool to help you orchestrate collaborative conversations with your students (Figure 2-20). (In *Chapter Three: Build Your Own HyperDoc*, you will find examples of these tools built into lessons.)

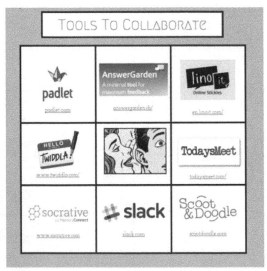

goo.gl/KE0w50

Figure 2-20

4 Vygotsky, L. S. Mind in Society: The Development of Higher Psychological Processes. Cambridge: Harvard University Press, 1978.

Connect

A digital educator explores new technology and connects with peers to share transformative ideas. A digital educator listens, contributes, solves problems, and inspires students, parents, colleagues, and administrators. A digital educator connects beyond his classroom, school, and district.

As you create HyperDocs, use web tools that allow your students to connect beyond the four walls of the classroom (Figure 2-21). In doing this, students will learn to have a local and global view of the world. Imagine exploring maps, commenting on and/or creating blogs, sharing student-produced videos, practicing speaking and listening skills through video conferencing, and using social media to connect and collaborate with classrooms around the world. Connecting with others will transform you as an educator.

And just as you are a digital connector, your students are, too. Together, you and your students can use any of the tools curated in the text set to connect with classrooms in your community and around the world, turning your traditional classroom into a *transformational* classroom. When you, the teacher, create, collaborate, and connect, you will not only meet the ISTE's standards for teachers and students, but you'll also give your students opportunities to do the previously inconceivable.

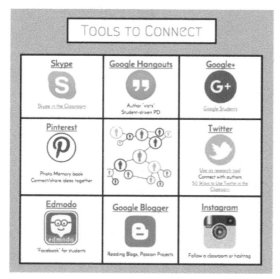

goo.gl/iOWZor

Figure 2-21

Critical Thinking

Including critical-thinking components in your HyperDoc that require students to go beyond the recall process, such as high-level questioning and open-ended tasks, is key to ensuring it's more than just a digital worksheet with links. From the types of questions you ask to the tasks you assign, critical thinking plays an important role throughout the HyperDoc's creation, collaboration, and connection processes. And though they're important, a HyperDoc is never just about the web tool you choose or the devices students work with—it is about how you craft your lesson. The text set includes many of our favorite websites and games, all of which give students an opportunity to strengthen their critical-thinking skills (Figure 2-22).

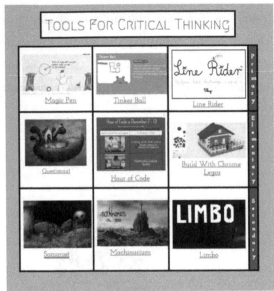

goo.gl/DmHg2E

Figure 2-22

Which Tool Is Best?

During the HyperDoc creation process, you'll need to determine which tools fit your needs best. Take the following into consideration:

- *If it's free*—We generally support the plethora of free web tools for educators, and we would never encourage a student to purchase one.

- *Teacher and student ease of use*—How will you teach with the tool? We encourage you and your students to play with web tools before using them to design content. Choose tools that work well on all of the devices available to you and your students.

- *If the web tool allows multiple collaborators*—Some tools allow for collaboration and some don't. When choosing your tool, consider the ease of collaboration.

- ***How easy it is for students to save their work***—Can students easily create, save, and access their designs using the web tool? Can students quickly save their work and turn it in to you? You'll find many edtech tools allow students to log in and save their work.

- ***Student privacy, data, and your responsibilities***—This area is quickly changing, so it's imperative that you always follow your district's policies on app and website usage to ensure you're abiding by federal and state legal requirements.

- ***Changes in technology***—Instead of focusing your HyperDoc on a particular tool, focus your HyperDoc on transformative pedagogy such as using the tool to connect, collaborate, and create. Tools are always evolving, and that dynamic nature lends itself beautifully to featuring different web tools and apps in your digital lesson plans.

- ***What can I do now that I couldn't before?*** This is the ultimate question to ask yourself as you determine which web tools to use in a more transformative way. Keep it in the back of your mind.

Because new companies are always launching and tools' capabilities are always changing, it can prove challenging to stay current with what's available. One way to keep up is by following Pinterest boards, specifically our Pinterest boards (Figure 2-23). We have organized our boards by subject as well as how you can integrate them into your lessons. Visit our boards to learn about new tools you can share with your students, whether you are assigning one tool or curating several so your students can collaborate, create, and connect. Visit our Pinterest page (Pinterest.com/tsgivets) and watch for new ideas to incorporate into your lessons.

goo.gl/F26SGj

Figure 2-23

A HyperDoc Creator's Learning Progression

We have created a HyperDoc learning progression detailing the transformation process educators go through as they strive for "heroism" in their classrooms (Figure 2-24). We know you're busy and won't be able to create a HyperDoc for every lesson plan, every day, and that's okay. As you move forward in your HyperDoc learning progression and explore new web tools, package lessons differently, and connect with other HyperDoc users, you'll see your classroom shift and your confidence grow. We hope you also support your colleagues wherever they are in their learning progression.

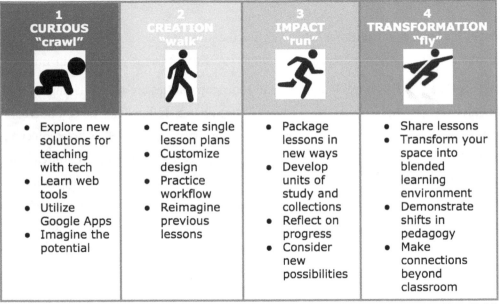

1 CURIOUS "crawl"	2 CREATION "walk"	3 IMPACT "run"	4 TRANSFORMATION "fly"
• Explore new solutions for teaching with tech • Learn web tools • Utilize Google Apps • Imagine the potential	• Create single lesson plans • Customize design • Practice workflow • Reimagine previous lessons	• Package lessons in new ways • Develop units of study and collections • Reflect on progress • Consider new possibilities	• Share lessons • Transform your space into blended learning environment • Demonstrate shifts in pedagogy • Make connections beyond classroom

Figure 2-24

Stage One: Curious

Like a baby learning to crawl and take in the new world, as a new HyperDoc user, you're curious about how to make learning more innovative. You may ask yourself: "My district just adopted Google Apps for Education—how can I effectively use them? Which web tools are appropriate for my grade level and content? How can Chromebooks help us meet *every* student's needs?" At this stage, you may want to identify a need first and then look for a solution, giving you a launchpad for reaching out, beginning to explore tools, and imagining the potential of HyperDocs.

Stage Two: Creation

After "crawling" around and exploring the technology world, you're now ready to stand on your own two feet and begin "walking" through the creation process. Most often, teachers will enter the HyperDoc gateway by creating multimedia text sets (pre-collected content), a simple way for creating and packaging lessons that will build your confidence (Figure 2-25). During this stage, you'll learn how to deliver your lessons in new ways by pushing out HyperDocs to your learners. You may also begin to create single lesson plans, customize Docs, and become more curious about technology's potential for your classroom. If you become frustrated at some point, remember that this is how students sometimes feel when they attempt something new, something outside of their comfort zone.

goo.gl/F26SGj

Figure 2-25

Stage Three: Impact

Now you're ready to "run"! At this stage, you're rethinking the design of your lesson plans, creating study units in HyperDocs, developing collections of lessons centered around a topic or theme, trying different Google Apps to package lessons, and considering new ways to encourage student learning through technology. You may also start seeing an effect on your students and their families, your colleagues, and perhaps even yourself. We've noticed that at this point teachers often become self-reflective and start to see how using HyperDocs is allowing them to work face-to-face with more students and re-engage with the curriculum. Observing your students' experiences will further motivate you to ask yourself, "What has HyperDocs allowed me to do now that I couldn't do before?"

Stage Four: Transformation

Congratulations—you're ready to "fly"! At this point, you should be confident in your ability to create HyperDocs, but still pushing yourself to develop lessons in new ways. You'll see shifts in your pedagogy, and your classroom will more closely resemble a blended learning environment. You will also begin to connect with other teachers and share your lessons through Twitter, Pinterest, and Facebook so you can help the HyperDoc community grow. Your confidence and competency will continue to improve as you join other teachers implementing this highly transformative method of instruction!

Be a Connected Learner!

Post a link to your HyperDoc on these social media sites:

twitter.com/TsGiveTs   pinterest.com/tsgivets   facebook.com/groups/HyperDocs

Our dream for HyperDocs is that teachers will create and use them to transform education from one-dimensional classrooms, in which the students sit and get information from a teacher and occasionally interact with one another, to a multidimensional classroom. In this multidimensional environment, teachers facilitate riveting experiences for students to create, connect, collaborate, and think critically about the world and their ideas. With HyperDocs, students (and the teachers themselves) are eager to learn. This could translate to taking a tried-and-true lesson plan and making it more interactive using the tips, tricks, and strategies described in this handbook, creating brand new lesson plans on a HyperDoc, or inviting students to create their own digital lesson plans. The next section in this handbook will break down the steps to building your own personalized HyperDocs.

Resources

Catlin Tucker, *Blended Learning in Grades 4-12*, (Corwin, 2012).
Alice Keeler and Libbi Miller, *50 Things You Can Do With Google Classroom*, (Dave Burgess Consulting, Inc., 2016)
Ruben R. Puentedura, "SAMR A Brief Introduction," Hippasus.com, October 14, 2015, http://hippasus.com/rrpweblog/archives/2015/10/SAMR_ABriefIntro.pdf.
"Standards for Teachers," Accessed March 2016, http://www.iste.org/standards/ISTE-standards/standards-for-teachers.

Heather Marshall,
@MsMarshallCMS
ELA and media teacher

"The world is changing at a rapid pace, and textbooks cannot always keep up."

"HyperDocs have allowed me to **personalize the learning experience** for my students by giving them the keys to drive on their own inquiry based journey. Before creating HyperDocs I was in control and we all did everything together at the same time because we were working from a lesson plan document that I kept to myself. By *repackaging this plan* and handing it over to the students in HyperDoc format I was able to **change the entire dynamic of my class.** The students were now in the driver's seat and in control of their own pace, spending as much time as they needed on something and deciding when to move on. Putting the students in control gives them a choice in what they will learn and how they will learn it, which has *increased student engagement tremendously.* Gone are the days of teaching the same lesson, in the same way, class after class. A carefully crafted HyperDoc can take many forms, allowing me to lay out a path before my students that can take their learning to **multiple destinations based on their interests** rather than accepting information as I present it to them.

HyperDocs can easily be modified or updated as new discoveries are made, which allows me to present my students with current information that is **relevant to their own lives.** With HyperDocs we don't have to get our information from a single source which might be an outdated textbook. **The world is changing at a rapid pace, and textbooks cannot always keep up.**

HyperDocs have also changed my role in the classroom, personalizing the learning of the students. Putting the learning in the hands of the students has freed me to be a part of their learning in a very different way; having conversations about learning, discussing ideas about creation and joining the class by commenting on shared digital content. I am really enjoying the way that my interactions with students have changed. **Our conversations about learning are taking place one-on-one,** rather than as a whole class address. I am no longer the only person that sees their work, and this has had a big impact on the quality of what my students produce because they care far more about their friends' opinions about what they have done. Now that their work has gone public, it seems to be more meaningful to them. **HyperDocs were the vehicle that brought us to this new level of collaborative learning.**

By putting the road map for our learning in the student's hands, I have become a passenger on their journey. They are no longer sitting in the backseat, staring blankly out the window and asking, "Are we there yet?" With my lesson plan as the road map and the HyperDoc as the vehicle, **student learning has become a series of epic road trips.** When was the last time anyone said that about a textbook?"

Build Your Own HyperDoc
3

In this section, we'll highlight what you can do with a HyperDoc and look at samples that feature the elements of good teaching, including blended learning, different web tools, learning modalities, and classroom management. We also want to share with you some of our favorite (current) tools and help you to imagine your own HyperDoc's possibilities. Our collection of methods for building HyperDocs is ever changing and ever growing. Each day, we receive emails and Tweets from teachers around the country who are creating digital lessons, each chock-full of creativity and design potential. In this chapter, we have captured just *some* of the ways you can utilize apps and web tools when building your own lesson. We hope this section sparks your own creativity, gives you an idea or two, and helps you envision the possibilities for *your own* HyperDoc.

We designed the basic HyperDoc template with the fundamentals of effective lesson design (engage, explore, explain, apply, share, reflect, and extend) in mind, but in no way does it reflect everything you can do. In fact, as you'll see, the HyperDoc parts we're sharing with you look very different from this template—and that's the point. Although you may start with a template, you won't end there. In fact, we actually hope you will think of things we have *not* included in this book and share them with us!

So what can you do with a HyperDoc?

TITLE
Brief Description/Outcome

	Engage
	{insert video, quote, other inspirational hook}

	Explore
	{insert instructional video, multimedia text sets, etc.}

	Explain
	{insert tool for students to collaborate on ideas}

	Apply
	{insert space for students to create, draft, etc.}

	Share
	{tool to create something, assessment evidence}

	Reflect
	{insert enrichment links, extra activities}

	Extend
	{insert enrichment links, extra activities}

Engage

First impressions matter, and using a HyperDoc to engage your class as you begin a lesson can be the key to capturing their attention, inspiring their curiosity, and building their excitement. Imagine drawing your students into a unit with an audio podcast, all the while building their background knowledge, or showing the perfect video to create a metaphor for your learning objectives, or sharing an image or quote that inspires thinking. This is the piece of the HyperDoc that gets your students walking into class asking, "What do we get to do today?" And whether you're planning a whole-class experience or an individual task, clearly label your expectations at the beginning of the HyperDoc to add structure and accountability and set the tone for the rest of your lesson. This doesn't have to be complicated or time consuming; rather, it can be as simple as "Turn and talk" or "Share your thinking with the person next to you."

Engage Tool: YouTube

YouTube is an incredible sharing platform for video and multimedia. Videos can engage students in learning by introducing an idea or concept and promoting curiosity and questioning while building the student's background knowledge of the topic.

Four Cs

Communication
Critical Thinking
Creativity
Collaboration

ISTE Standards

Creativity and Innovation
Technology Operations
Digital Citizenship
Critical Thinking
Research and Information
Communication and Collaboration

DOK

Level 1—Recall
Level 2—Skills/Concepts
Level 3—Strategic Thinking
Level 4—Extended Thinking

SAMR

Substitution
Augmentation
Modification
Redefinition

goo.gl/S9vSxe

How to Design

- Find a video that inspires you and fits your lesson's objectives.
- Link to the video in the HyperDoc.

How to Deliver

Videos can be shown to the whole group or packaged in a HyperDoc for each student to view independently. Choose parts of the video on which to pause and promote student thinking.

How to Collect

In a blended learning classroom, students can record their responses in a writer's notebook or on paper.

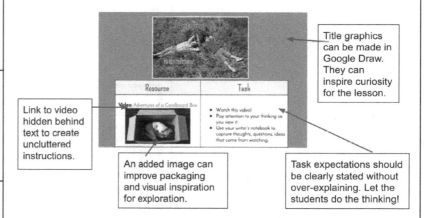

Title graphics can be made in Google Draw. They can inspire curiosity for the lesson.

Link to video hidden behind text to create uncluttered instructions.

An added image can improve packaging and visual inspiration for exploration.

Task expectations should be clearly stated without over-explaining. Let the students do the thinking!

Engage Tool: Podcasts

When you introduce a concept as audio during the engagement phase of a lesson, students improve their listening comprehension skills while gaining important background knowledge about the topic. Use your favorite podcasts or check out ListenCurrent.com which features free podcasts focused on social studies, science, English language arts, and current events. You can link to any of these podcasts in any HyperDoc

Four Cs

Communication
Critical Thinking
Creativity
Collaboration

ISTE Standards

Creativity and Innovation
Technology Operations
Digital Citizenship
Critical Thinking
Research and Information
Communication and Collaboration

DOK

Level 1—Recall
Level 2—Skills/Concepts
Level 3—Strategic Thinking
Level 4—Extended Thinking

SAMR

Substitution
Augmentation
Modification
Redefinition

goo.gl/ttdQuv

How to Design

• Explore the topics on Listen Current's website that best align with your lesson's objectives.

• Link to a podcast in the HyperDoc and state your expectations for listening.

How to Deliver

Students can listen to a podcast during class time individually, in small groups, or as a whole class. A benefit to linking to a podcast is that students can access the content and listen again at any point in the lesson.

How to Collect

For this lesson, give students a prompt to consider while listening to the podcast so they can prepare for the subsequent class discussion and debate.

Introduction	Your Task
Aa ELA Middle School **'The Giver' and Memory**	• Listen to the podcast linked on the left in class. (Listen again if you want, post-class-listening.)
"The Giver" is a story about a world without memories. A new movie version of the novel depicts this world as a sterile, emotionless place. In this story, public radio talks with author Lois Lowry and how she came up with the idea to write the book. The book asks, "wouldn't it be easier if we didn't have memories?"	• Think about: *Would it be easier if we didn't have memories?*
Fiction Science Fiction Fantasy	
Listen Current: The Giver and Memory	

Engage Tool: Images

Engage students in a topic by using images to build curiosity, share background information, and generate lists of questions. Students practice their visual literacy by viewing images and answering basic questions about what they see.

Four Cs

Communication
Critical Thinking
Creativity
Collaboration

ISTE Standards

Creativity and Innovation
Technology Operations
Digital Citizenship
Critical Thinking
Research and Information
Communication and Collaboration

DOK

Level 1—Recall
Level 2—Skills/Concepts
Level 3—Strategic Thinking
Level 4—Extended Thinking

SAMR

Substitution
Augmentation
Modification
Redefinition

goo.gl/u4foLH

How to Design

- Choose an image that relates to your HyperDoc's topic.
- Add the image to a Google Form and prompt students to answer questions.

How to Deliver

- Students view the form and complete the questions.
- Share students' responses from the Sheet linked to the form.

How to Collect

Students engage in sharing their ideas, prior knowledge, and questions about the topic during the class discussion.

BONUS: *The New York Times* and *The Learning Network* host "What's Going On in This Picture?" (goo.gl/PqE7D0)

Each Monday, an interesting photo and the following three questions are posted:

- What is going on in this picture?
- What do you see that makes you say that?
- What more can you find?

Students can comment and reply to comments in the public comment forum. Elevate this lesson on the SAMR model from modification to redefinition by having students communicate in the forum and interact with the public's comments.

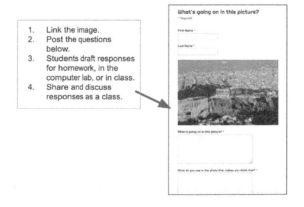

Engage Tool: Memes

A meme is an image, video, or piece of text that has been imitated and then tweaked to be humorous. Using humor in the classroom is a great way to connect with students and engage them in a topic that might not be inherently interesting to them. It is also important to be culturally responsive to our learners, and memes are a fun, trendy way to communicate an idea. Meme Generator (MemeGenerator.net) is one tool you can use to create your own memes, although it is certainly not the only one. So go ahead and get your funny on!

Four Cs

Communication
Critical Thinking
Creativity
Collaboration

ISTE Standards

Creativity and Innovation
Technology Operations
Digital Citizenship
Critical Thinking
Research and Information
Communication and Collaboration

DOK

Level 1—Recall
Level 2—Skills/Concepts
Level 3—Strategic Thinking
Level 4—Extended Thinking

SAMR

Substitution
Augmentation
Modification
Redefinition

goo.gl/iQEAhe

How to Design

• Once you are at MemeGenerator.net, upload your own image, search pre-made memes, or use a template to create a meme.

• Add text to your image, whether you have uploaded your own image or used a template.

How to Deliver

When used as an engagement tool, you will often see a meme at the beginning of the lesson. The following example shows how you can use a meme to connect with students.

How to Collect

You can choose to collect the student thinking during class discussion or through comments written on a Google Doc.

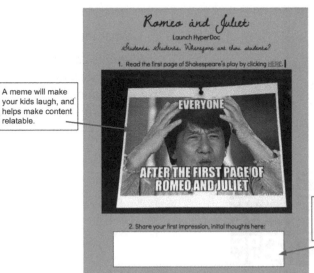

A meme will make your kids laugh, and helps make content relatable.

This brief activity will 1) connect students 2) serve as baseline data for the teacher.

Engage Tool: Quotes

Sometimes we want to spark our students' curiosity and engage them in conversation. One way to do this is by putting a catchy or thought-provoking quote on a Google Slide and then soliciting your students' thoughts through AnswerGarden (AnswerGarden.ch).

Four Cs

Communication
Critical Thinking
Creativity
Collaboration

ISTE Standards

Creativity and Innovation
Technology Operations
Digital Citizenship
Critical Thinking
Research and Information
Communication and Collaboration

DOK

Level 1—Recall
Level 2—Skills/Concepts
Level 3—Strategic Thinking
Level 4—Extended Thinking

SAMR

Substitution
Augmentation
Modification
Redefinition

goo.gl/O5KSxU

How to Design

- Choose a quote.
- Copy the quote onto a Google Slide.
- From the slide, link to a reflective question posted to AnswerGarden.

How to Deliver

Share the slide and invite participants to respond to the quote using the AnswerGarden web tool. Here is an example where teachers attending a professional-development session were invited to reflect on a quote using one word. Afterward, as a whole group, the teachers discussed the most popular word(s) gathered in the AnswerGarden word cloud.

How to Collect

As the responses are posted, watch the AnswerGarden word cloud grow. Words or themes used most often stand out in a larger font, which can be a starting point to understanding the group's thinking or the content's theme.

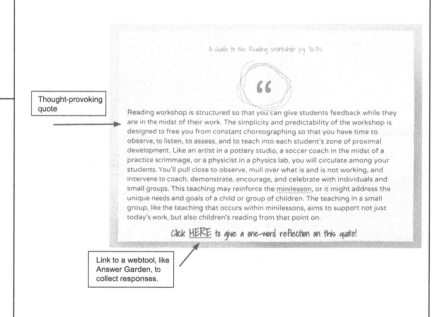

Thought-provoking quote

Link to a webtool, like Answer Garden, to collect responses.

Explore

Once the stage is set and your class is engaged, offer your students time to more thoroughly explore a topic by providing them with an exploration activity in your HyperDoc. You can start preparing for this portion of the lesson early on by collecting your favorite resource links that promote thought and ignite curiosity. As they explore, students will begin learning about the topic, forming their own opinions, and asking questions. And because students have countless resources readily available at their fingertips, they tend to dive into a rabbit hole and become so immersed in the information they're finding that they don't want to stop exploring. Of course, this excitement is also one of the many benefits of creating exploration time. Don't be too surprised if your students continue exploring the topic at their own pace at home or at school and begin finding their own favorite links to information about your topic to explore. In fact, you may even consider adding a section to your HyperDoc where students can share their newly discovered resources with one another.

Allowing time for students to explore and share their ideas about a topic before launching into a specific learning objective creates a curious classroom community that's willing to take risks and ask questions.

Explore Tool: Multimedia Text Sets

A multimedia text set is a collection of text about a topic that includes a variety of information sources such as websites, articles, videos, images, quotes, and infographics. Students explore the collection of resources and are immersed in the various perspectives presented on the same topic. Exploring a multimedia text set requires that students practice their digital literacy skills and build schema on the topic.

Four Cs

Communication
Critical Thinking
Creativity
Collaboration

ISTE Standards

Creativity and Innovation
Technology Operations
Digital Citizenship
Critical Thinking
Research and Information
Communication and Collaboration

DOK

Level 1—Recall
Level 2—Skills/Concepts
Level 3—Strategic Thinking
Level 4—Extended Thinking

SAMR

Substitution
Augmentation
Modification
Redefinition

goo.gl/r2EdCV

How to Design

• Insert a two-column table in a Google Doc.

• In one column, link students to a resource.

• In the second column, create a way for students to respond to a broader question, record their thinking, and/or take notes.

How to Deliver

Share the Doc with students. When students click on the linked resources in the table, a new tab will pop up in the web browser with teacher-selected text. In the new tab, students read and explore the link. Students then record their notes in the Google Doc.

How to Collect

Through Google Classroom:

• Create an assignment in Google Classroom.

• Select the option to make a copy for each student so you can collect individual student data.

• Provide feedback in the Doc.

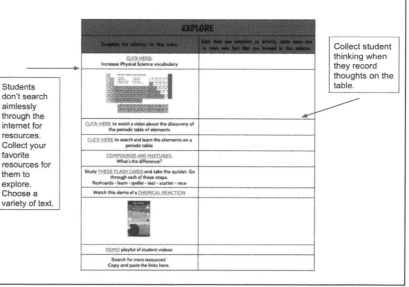

Students don't search aimlessly through the internet for resources. Collect your favorite resources for them to explore. Choose a variety of text.

Collect student thinking when they record thoughts on the table.

Explore Tool: YouTube Playlists

After students have read an article or text excerpt about a topic, give them visual content so they can explore further. Watching videos helps improve a student's understanding of the topic at hand, while offering students who need this type of visual and auditory support easier access to your curriculum.

When you invite students to explore a topic through videos, it helps to pre-curate the content by creating a YouTube (YouTube.com) playlist. You can then link students to your playlist in your HyperDoc, allowing them to quickly access and explore the content on their own or with a classmate.

Four Cs

Communication
Critical Thinking
Creativity
Collaboration

ISTE Standards

Creativity and Innovation
Technology Operations
Digital Citizenship
Critical Thinking
Research and Information
Communication and Collaboration

DOK

Level 1—Recall
Level 2—Skills/Concepts
Level 3—Strategic Thinking
Level 4—Extended Thinking

SAMR

Substitution
Augmentation
Modification
Redefinition

goo.gl/e9z0FQ

How to Design

- Create a new YouTube playlist featuring relevant videos for your students to explore.
- In your HyperDoc, state your expectations for students as they watch the videos. Will they respond to a prompt after they watch the video? Discuss a new discovery with classmates? Or will they just explore for the sake of exploring?

How to Deliver

(This is a blended learning lesson.)
Include a link to your YouTube playlist in your HyperDoc. As students watch the videos, they will take notes in a notebook.

How to Collect

Depending on what you expect from the exploration time, you can collect student thinking in multiple ways:

- Anecdotal records based on conversations (formative assessment)
- Student responses in a notebook
- A collection form where students submit videos they have found.

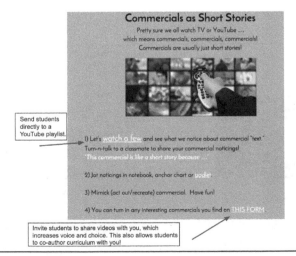

Explore Tool: ThingLink

ThingLink (ThingLink.com) is the perfect web tool for building background knowledge through exploration. The website allows you to upload an image and then add "hot spots," which are areas that a viewer clicks to learn more information. Students choose the order in which they explore the content, inspiring curiosity and developing their inquiry-based learning skills.

Four Cs

Communication
Critical Thinking
Creativity
Collaboration

ISTE Standards

Creativity and Innovation
Technology Operations
Digital Citizenship
Critical Thinking
Research and Information
Communication and Collaboration

DOK

Level 1—Recall
Level 2—Skills/Concepts
Level 3—Strategic Thinking
Level 4—Extended Thinking

SAMR

Substitution
Augmentation
Modification
Redefinition

goo.gl/hg0nCE   goo.gl/sKTfyH

How to Design

You can either create your own content or explore and choose from ThingLink's extensive database of photos and videos (thinglink.com).

- Find an image, upload it, and add links to vocabulary words, videos relating to the content, or links to a great article.

How to Deliver

If you've created your HyperDoc using a Google Doc, link a ThingLink or embed your ThingLink in a website HyperDoc. As students hover over the image, the designated hot spots will appear. Students can then click the links that appear or simply read the content that pops up.

How to Collect

Add a Google Form directly to a ThingLink so you can instantly collect student thinking as they complete their exploration, all in one location. Or you may prompt students to record their new knowledge in their notebooks or on a piece of paper to turn in.

Explore Tool: Google My Maps

To help students develop a curiosity for learning, we must provide them opportunities to explore their interests. Creating personalized Google My Maps is one way to do just this. Using this web tool, you can actually "plant" content where it took place on a map and then post corresponding text, images, videos, and links to take students to the next portion of the assignment. For example, if you were to drop a pin on Mount St. Helens, your students could view a video of the volcano erupting and then zoom in on the map to see the actual scarring left on the earth. Google My Maps' pins encourage students to determine their learning's pace and path and engages their curiosity so they want to see what the next pin has in store. As students progress, you could add another layer to this powerful learning tool by having them create their own maps.

Four Cs

Communication
Critical Thinking
Creativity
Collaboration

ISTE Standards

Creativity and Innovation
Technology Operations
Digital Citizenship
Critical Thinking
Research and Information
Communication and Collaboration

DOK

Level 1—Recall
Level 2—Skills/Concepts
Level 3—Strategic Thinking
Level 4—Extended Thinking

SAMR

Substitution
Augmentation
Modification
Redefinition

goo.gl/jSsFqU

How to Design

- On your Google Apps for Education Drive, select New and then My Maps.
- Create a personal Google My Map. Add locations by placing markers in strategic places.
- Post the content you want students to discover for each location.
- In this example, created by Vidya Kumar, students explored a biography of the life of Martin Luther King, Jr., by exploring the map.

How to Deliver

Embed your map or share its link on a Google Site. Discuss how to explore the map to not only learn its content, but also how to view it as a mentor text. Students will eventually create their own personalized map, highlighting important events relating to their report's subject.

How to Collect

After exploring the map, discuss the elements of a biography and how to use Google My Maps. This prepares students for the application step later on in the lesson when they'll create their own biography map.

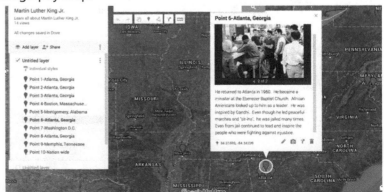

Explain

Now that your learners are engaged and have had a chance to explore, it's time for the one-two punch: "Bam! This is what I want you to learn." Traditionally, teachers stand in front of the classroom and deliver content in the form of a lecture to their students, who are then expected to retain the information. Occasionally, teachers will use visuals to enhance their explanation or teach the content in another way. We encourage you, though, to shy away from spending too much time as the "sage on the stage" and become more of a "guide on the side."

Part of the reason why a HyperDoc is both teacher- and student-friendly is that your explanation can include instructional videos, online articles, step-by-step blog posts, or an application, making your direct instruction more engaging. Planning a HyperDoc's explanation section allows you, as the teacher, to carefully consider your content delivery as well as how your students will revisit it. For example, some HyperDocs have a built-in explanation, while others provide students links to access content on the Internet. Either way, HyperDocs let you embed your direct instruction in more creative, engaging ways so that your students can access it again and again.

Explain Tool: Google Docs and Chrome Extensions

Google Chrome extensions are effective, easy-to-add tools that can help you meet your students' specific learning needs. Case in point: If a student comprehends text better when it's read aloud, he could install the Read&Write (goo.gl/FXentO) extension in Google Chrome, and it would read the online text to him. Then, in the Google Doc, he could use the highlighting tools to make note of important text and use the comment features to annotate the Doc with his thinking.

Four Cs

Communication
Critical Thinking
Creativity
Collaboration

ISTE Standards

Creativity and Innovation
Technology Operations
Digital Citizenship
Critical Thinking
Research and Information
Communication and Collaboration

DOK

Level 1—Recall
Level 2—Skills/Concepts
Level 3—Strategic Thinking
Level 4—Extended Thinking

SAMR

Substitution
Augmentation
Modification
Redefinition

goo.gl/S47uyp

How to Design

- Choose an interesting article or text relating to your learning objectives for students to read.
- Paste the text from the article into a Google Doc, making sure to link to the original text and cite your sources.
- Add directions for reading the text above the article.
- Include links to a screencast or video for inserting Google Chrome extensions (as needed).

How to Deliver

- Link directions from the HyperDoc with clear expectations.

Should Native Americans Be Mascots?	
ENGAGE	Watch THIS VIDEO as a whole group. During the video, students respond to the questions about the video on THIS FORM.
EXPLORE	CLICK HERE to view the student responses. Discuss as a class. Start forming your opinion about whether or not Native Americans should be mascots.
EXPLAIN	CLICK HERE for further reading. Record your thinking on the Doc and collect data for a discussion.
APPLY	Time to take a stand! List the thinking below for both sides of the debate. Consider both sides of the debate. At the end of this discussion, you will be asked to choose a side of the argument.

- Students make a copy of the document and place it on their Google Drive.
- Students then follow the directions according to the Doc.

Explain Tool: Google Docs and Chrome Extensions

Use screencast directions to explain how to insert the Chrome Extension.

1. Watch *THIS VIDEO* ~ Follow the video directions to add the *READ & WRITE FOR GOOGLE* Chrome Extension
2. You will read this article 3 times to practice CLOSE READING. Each time you read, read with a different lens listed below:
   a. First read ~ use the Chrome extension to listen while the text is read aloud
   b. Second read ~ highlight new vocabulary and define words in the comment section of the document
   c. Third read ~ record your thinking in the comments section of the text
3. Use your document comment annotations to support your thinking during the class debate.

TRIBE WANTS TOWN TO KEEP NATIVE AMERICAN ON ITS LOGO

By The Record, adapted by Newsela staff ~ 07.28.14

Utilize Google Doc tools such as highlighting and comments to annotate text.

How to Collect

Depending upon your expectations, you can collect your students' thinking in multiple ways, including:

- Anecdotal records based on class discussion

- Student-annotated notes or responses in a Google Doc

Explain Tool: Video Instruction

Strategically placing an instructional video in a HyperDoc gives your students access to an "explanation" when they need it, supporting their learning process. And when combined with direct instruction, students can instantly "replay" the day's lesson at their own pace and on their own schedule. This is perfect if a student is absent and misses the lesson or needs to hear a concept more than once.

Note: For classrooms with limited devices, students can share as needed. The expectation is not for the explanation portion to be done outside of the classroom, but it can be.

Four Cs

Communication
Critical Thinking
Creativity
Collaboration

ISTE Standards

Creativity and Innovation
Technology Operations
Digital Citizenship
Critical Thinking
Research and Information
Communication and Collaboration

DOK

Level 1—Recall
Level 2—Skills/Concepts
Level 3—Strategic Thinking
Level 4—Extended Thinking

SAMR

Substitution
Augmentation
Modification
Redefinition

goo.gl/0Fk8P2

How to Design

You can choose to use a pre-made instructional video from YouTube, Khan Academy (KhanAcademy.org), or TED-Ed (ed.Ted.com), or you can create your own.

- For web-based content or instructions, use screencasting tools such as Screencast-O-Matic (Screencast-O-Matic.com) Techsmith's Snagit (Techsmith.com/snagit), and QuickTime (Apple.com/quicktime: Mac users).

- Doceri (Doceri.com), Explain Everything (ExplainEverything.com), and Educreations (Educreations.com) are great apps for creating whiteboard-type videos.

- EDpuzzle (edpuzzle.com) allows you to create interactive videos and includes accountablity features.

- Keep your videos to a maximum of three minutes and be sure not to use them as substitutions for longer lectures.

How to Deliver

Place a link to your video in the HyperDoc next to the section where the instruction is needed. This prevents the student having to take time and search for what he needs to complete his assigned tasks. If you're using Google Slides, Forms, Sites, or My Maps to package the HyperDoc, the video tutorial can be embedded directly into the page.

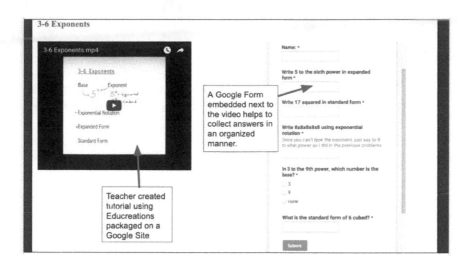

How to Collect

Sometimes a video will simply be a resource for aiding instruction, while other times it will be a way to check in with your students and assess their comprehension of a topic. Creating a Google Form is one convenient method for doing just this because you can either place a video directly in the form or next to it if the video is embedded on a Google Site. This also helps with grading because all of your students' responses will be collected in one spreadsheet.

Explain Tool: Tween Tribune + Google Docs and Tables

Tween Tribune (TweenTribune.com) features articles about current events organized by Lexile and grade level. The website's articles also include education-related questions and align to national standards. In the following sample HyperDoc, the teaching objective was that students would be able to identify a news article's key ideas. In this explain activity, modeled as a shared experience with the class, students can apply and practice the skill of independently reading nonfiction text closely. This HyperDoc is a perfect go-to sub plan.

Four Cs

Communication
Critical Thinking
Creativity
Collaboration

ISTE Standards

Creativity and Innovation
Technology Operations
Digital Citizenship
Critical Thinking
Research and Information
Communication and Collaboration

DOK

Level 1—Recall
Level 2—Skills/Concepts
Level 3—Strategic Thinking
Level 4—Extended Thinking

SAMR

Substitution
Augmentation
Modification
Redefinition

goo.gl/gtld9z

How to Design

- On your Google Doc, include a link to the Tween Tribune article
- Create a table in the Google Doc.
- Add the reading skills or questions you want students to complete.

How to Deliver

You probably want your students reading articles on a regular basis, so you'll use this HyperDoc more than once in your classroom. Possible methods of delivery:

- Have students independently read and respond in the HyperDoc if you have delivered the assignment in Google Classroom.
- Invite students to work with partners or in small groups using one device.
- Once your students are familiar with a delivery method, this HyperDoc makes for easy substitute plans.

How to Collect

The easiest way to collect student thinking is to assign the document in Google Classroom so the program can make a copy for each student. Give immediate feedback to individual students while they are working on the assignment.

Quick Tip: Walk students through these workflow steps before they complete the assignment so you can monitor their progress in real time.

Explain Tool: Tween Tribune + Google Docs and Tables

Clear directions on the document explain to students what steps to take to complete the assignment. The content of the article or the questions on the table explain to students the learning objective.

Developing Comprehension in a Digital World
Nonfiction Notes

1. Go to the website, http://tweentribune.com/
2. Sign in as a student. Use your school gmail and password. Log into my classroom. It is called Mrs. Hilton's Classroom - 5th grade
3. Choose an interesting article to read.
4. Read the article and fill out the information about the article below. Be specific and use complete sentences when you respond.

Students write responses in this column.

Student task is listed in one column with the learning objectives.

Title of text:	
Copy the URL link to the article here:	
Take notes while you are reading the article:	
WHO is the article mostly about?	
WHAT is the main event of the article?	
WHERE does the story take place?	
WHEN is the event happening?	
WHY is this article important? BIG IDEA!!	
Take the Tween Tribune quiz online about the article. If you can, record your quiz score here.	
Find another article that interests you. Post the url links to the articles that you read.	

Explain Tool: YouTube Playlists

YouTube has a great catalog of videos that can help you explain topics in an engaging, fun way. To collect and organize your favorite videos, create a playlist that you can update and share with your students each year.

Four Cs

Communication
Critical Thinking
Creativity
Collaboration

ISTE Standards

Creativity and Innovation
Technology Operations
Digital Citizenship
Critical Thinking
Research and Information
Communication and Collaboration

DOK

Level 1—Recall
Level 2—Skills/Concepts
Level 3—Strategic Thinking
Level 4—Extended Thinking

SAMR

Substitution
Augmentation
Modification
Redefinition

goo.gl/rnhDH0

How to Design

Identify the main topics covered using your textbook or unit's content guide and then search and preview videos for each of the topics, adding them to a specific playlist you have created as you go. Ensure you have two to three videos per topic and arrange them in the order covered in your unit.

How to Deliver

Share your YouTube playlist with students by either linking to it or embedding it directly in a Google Site. Alternatively, to give students easier access to your videos rather than sending them to YouTube, link your playlist of instructional videos to slides in a Google Slides presentation or embed individual videos on a Slide for students to view and respond to in a slide book.

How to Collect

Whether you're using a blended learning approach and having students record their thinking on paper or you're going digital and encouraging collaboration, clearly state, label, and post your expectations and instructions.

Explain Tool: YouTube Playlists

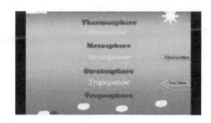

Weather

by highfillcrew • 14 videos • 846 views • Last u

▶ Play all   < Share   + Save

1 — **The Atmosphere - All you need to know**
by WeatherSchool

2 — **Bill Nye The Science Guy on The Atmosphere (Full Clip)**
by Bill Nye

3 — Layers of the Atmosphere.mov
by Mr. G

4 — **Reveal Earth's Atmosphere**
by National Geographic

5 — **Bill Nye The Science Guy on Wind (Full Clip)**
by Bill Nye

6 — **Earth's Tilt and the Seasons - for Planetarium Show**
by Brad Freese

7 — **Our World: What is Weather?**
by NASAeClips

8 — **Our World: What is a Cloud?**
by NASAeClips

Explain Tool: Google Slides Books

There are more uses for a Google Slides presentation than just giving speeches—in fact, it's actually the perfect tool to use for packaging content. Keeping in mind copyright laws and proper citation practices, you can use Google Slides to create interactive digital textbooks that engage and educate your students through links, videos, and images that appear right alongside the text. The possibilities are endless. And while creating the slides and content may fall to you at first, it can eventually become a great project for students.

Four Cs

Communication
Critical Thinking
Creativity
Collaboration

ISTE Standards

Creativity and Innovation
Technology Operations
Digital Citizenship
Critical Thinking
Research and Information
Communication and Collaboration

DOK

Level 1—Recall
Level 2—Skills/Concepts
Level 3—Strategic Thinking
Level 4—Extended Thinking

SAMR

Substitution
Augmenation
Modification
Redefinition

goo.gl/FQBZ0z   goo.gl/8HGDtE

How to Design

- Create a view-only Google Slides deck.
- Add images, text, and links to additional resources to the slides.
- If needed, include links to assessment questions.
- One more design idea: Some creators change the size of their slides to 8.5" by 11", mimicking the original page size for effect. Create a specific space for student input or note-taking and give students instructions for collaboration.

How to Deliver

You can share your Google Slides presentation by either linking to it or embedding it directly into a Google Site for easy access. Keep the deck view-only and instruct students to make a copy if you expect them to take notes directly on the slides. To collaborate, students can share copies of their slide decks with their classmates.

How to Collect

If a Google Slides presentation is for consumption only and you won't be assessing your students, don't worry about collecting anything. If you link to a Google Form in the slideshow to check your students' comprehension, there will again be no need to collect anything since the responses will automatically populate a spreadsheet. Often, you'll see slideshows that include space for student responses or group collaboration directly on the slides. In this case, students copy and share the slide deck with their teacher.

Explain Tool: Google Slides Books

Created by Matt Mcfarlane

Created by Rocky Logue

Explain Tool: EDpuzzle

EDpuzzle is a web tool that empowers teachers to turn any video into an engaging lesson. A teacher can crop a video, personalize with voiceovers, and embed quizzes at any time. If you don't want to create your own, you are sure to find one in the EDpuzzle gallery that already fits your needs.

Four Cs

Communication
Critical Thinking
Creativity
Collaboration

ISTE Standards

Creativity and Innovation
Technology Operations
Digital Citizenship
Critical Thinking
Research and Information
Communication and Collaboration

DOK

Level 1—Recall
Level 2—Skills/Concepts
Level 3—Strategic Thinking
Level 4—Extended Thinking

SAMR

Substitution
Augmentation
Modification
Redefinition

goo.gl/R099Aj

How to Design

EDpuzzle (edpuzzle.com) has an extensive database of video content that you are free to explore and use. Find a video that aligns with your lesson and customize it with voiceovers and questions to fit your needs, or you can create your own video!

How to Deliver

EDpuzzle allows you to invite students to the "classroom." You can even import a class from Google Classroom.

You can store your content and share it with multiple classes as well as assign a due date.

- Students will each receive their own EDpuzzle account, login, and questions to which they'll respond to while watching the video.

- In a blended learning classroom, you could use EDpuzzle during "centers," when students are cycling through a rotation of learning opportunities focused on a specific topic. This is an ideal scenario for classrooms with limited devices. For example, during a science lesson, you might have a quarter of the class reading from texts about tornados, another quarter creating their own tornado in a bottle, another quarter teaching a science partner about how a tornado forms, and the last quarter watching an interesting EDpuzzle video.

How to Collect

You can use your EDpuzzle teacher login to collect your students' responses to the video prompts.

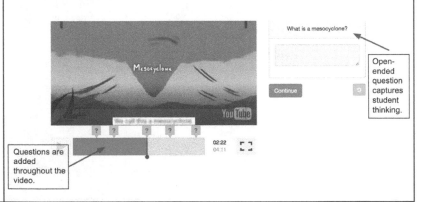

What is a mesocyclone?

Open-ended question captures student thinking.

Questions are added throughout the video.

Apply

Do your students consume technology or do they *create* it? We like to think that when a student consumes technology, the information goes from the computer to his brain, whereas when he creates it, ideas go from him to the computer. And although we often view learning as only taking place during the instructional portion of our lesson, deeper levels of synthesis actually occur during the apply phase. This is when students take the knowledge they've acquired and use it to create something.

As you design the apply portion of your HyperDoc, include learning opportunities that will encourage your students to develop their independent and critical thinking as well as problem-solving skills. As students digest and comprehend the lesson's content, allow them to use web tools to hone these skills and demonstrate what they've learned. If we want our students to be creative problem solvers, then we need to create opportunities for them to practice and develop these skills. Students often develop additional soft skills during the application process, including perseverance, teamwork, flexibility, and time management.

An Important Apply Tip for Teachers

When introducing a new tech tool, give your students time to play with it before requiring them to create something with it for an assessment. In fact, giving them time to explore the "how-to's" of a web tool using a low cognitive load is as much a part of the learning process as the product itself.

For example, have your students create something about themselves using the new tool. You could add a community-building layer to your classroom and ask them to share their creations. When it's time to produce a final product, the students will focus more on the content than struggling to figure out the tool. This could even become a valuable opportunity for students to reflect on and share how they resolved issues and figured out complicated tasks with little direct instruction, further developing their soft skills. This is when the real learning takes place, so it's worth taking the time to include and acknowledge.

Apply Tool: Google Story Builder

Google Story Builder allows you to create mini video stories. You can personalize the videos by using characters, story, and even music of your choosing. When finished, you can share your final product with others. Students reimagine a conversation, scene, or story between different characters, real or make-believe, such as Darth Vader and Luke Skywalker or Romeo and Juliet. Then they type the conversation in the tool that looks like a Google Doc. When it is time to publish, the conversation is read across a Google Doc with music and name-labeled cursors specifying the dialogue between the characters.

Four Cs

Communication
Critical Thinking
Creativity
Collaboration

ISTE Standards

Creativity and Innovation
Technology Operations
Digital Citizenship
Critical Thinking
Research and Information
Communication and Collaboration

DOK

Level 1—Recall
Level 2—Skills/Concepts
Level 3—Strategic Thinking
Level 4—Extended Thinking

SAMR

Substitution
Augmentation
Modification
Redefinition

goo.gl/opKCd9

How to Design

- Log in to Google Story Builder.
- Follow the steps presented on the HyperDoc.

Caution: Draft a conversation between two characters before you begin—you cannot go back and revise once you've started because the web tool does not save if you decide to go back a step.

How to Deliver

Start by sharing a link to your HyperDoc and instructing students to make a copy of the HyperDoc. Review the instructions as a class and, depending on the age of your students, run through a quick demo of how to create a Story Builder video. We've included a video tutorial that students can reference if they get stuck in the following HyperDoc example.

How to Collect

Using a Google Form to collect links to your students' Google Story Builder videos is the easiest way to keep student creations organized. Instruct students about how to find and copy the link at the end of the creation process so they can add it to the spreadsheet. This is also a great way for students to immediately share their projects with the entire class.

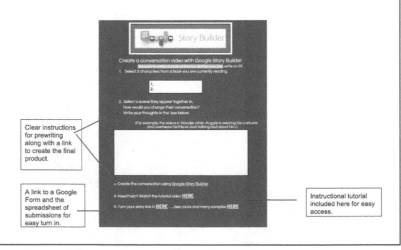

Apply Tool: PowToon

It's a fact: Kids love cartoons. Give your students an opportunity to create their own animated cartoon using PowToon (PowToon.com), and just watch as they come alive. PowToon, a comprehensive web tool, offers educators and students limited access for free accounts, templates, and video tutorials. Students can use PowToon's library of characters, settings, and icons (to ensure continuity), and even their own images and videos to create PowToons that demonstrate a synthesis of the lesson. They can also practice their fluency when they record their voices.

With guidelines and a rubric in place, a published PowToon could showcase a student's learning and be used as a formative assessment or on a report card.

Four Cs

Communication
Critical Thinking
Creativity
Collaboration

ISTE Standards

Creativity and Innovation
Technology Operations
Digital Citizenship
Critical Thinking
Research and Information
Communication and Collaboration

DOK

Level 1—Recall
Level 2—Skills/Concepts
Level 3—Strategic Thinking
Level 4—Extended Thinking

SAMR

Substitution
Augmentation
Modification
Redefinition

goo.gl/XQJ455

How to Design

- Set up a PowToon Educator Account. Share your login information with students through an email, in a Doc, or in a slide deck.

- Consider giving students time to play with the templates and explore PowToon before asking them to create a video for an assessment.

- Watch the tutorials together as a class and set up the learning objectives for the PowToon in a HyperDoc.

How to Deliver

Students create their PowToons in their own accounts. PowToon is not a collaborative tool, so if students are working in groups, they need to choose one account to use when creating their video.

How to Collect

Students publish their video and copy its URL into a Google Form, allowing them to share their work with you and their peers.

Quick Tip: Before you ask students to create a PowToon, make one yourself to showcase as a mentor video.

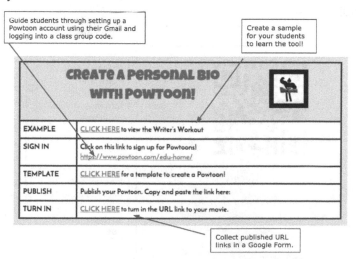

Guide students through setting up a Powtoon account using their Gmail and logging into a class group code.

Create a sample for your students to learn the tool!

CREATE A PERSONAL BIO WITH POWTOON!

EXAMPLE	CLICK HERE to view the Writer's Workout
SIGN IN	Click on this link to sign up for Powtoons! https://www.powtoon.com/edu-home/
TEMPLATE	CLICK HERE for a template to create a Powtoon!
PUBLISH	Publish your Powtoon. Copy and paste the link here:
TURN IN	CLICK HERE to turn in the URL link to your movie.

Collect published URL links in a Google Form.

Apply Tool: Show-What-You-Know Bingo

At the end of a unit, rather than grading multiple PowerPoint presentations, let your students decide which web tool would help them best show you what they learned. This added layer of decision is an important component in authentic critical-thinking activities. Plus, chances are, every student will choose from the variety offered.

Four Cs

Communication
Critical Thinking
Creativity
Collaboration

ISTE Standards

Creativity and Innovation
Technology Operations
Digital Citizenship
Critical Thinking
Research and Information
Communication and Collaboration

DOK

Level 1—Recall
Level 2—Skills/Concepts
Level 3—Strategic Thinking
Level 4—Extended Thinking

SAMR

Substitution
Augmentation
Modification
Redefinition

goo.gl/4wpPQk

How to Design

The Show-What-You-Know HyperDoc is widely shared, meant for everyone to use. Just open the document, click File, make a copy, and it's yours. Add or delete any web tools in the table so that it reflects the devices you have in your classroom.

How to Deliver

To share the HyperDoc, ensure your share settings are set to view-only, then post the link for students to access.

How to Collect

In the HyperDoc, change the link in the center of the table and add your own Google Form, where students will turn in their projects. In an effort to move away from presenting one project at a time, offer students the link to your spreadsheet so they can view everyone's work on their own. This enables all of your students to be engaged and learning at the same time—rather than passively listening, which takes valuable class time.

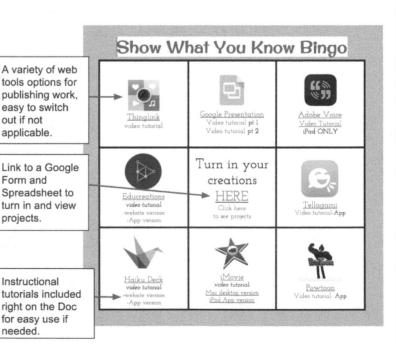

A variety of web tools options for publishing work, easy to switch out if not applicable.

Link to a Google Form and Spreadsheet to turn in and view projects.

Instructional tutorials included right on the Doc for easy use if needed.

Apply Tool: Storybird

From reading others' published work to creating their own poems, picture books, and chapter stories, Storybird (Storybird.com) offers students of all ages a variety of resources, all in one location. Storybird can inspire even your most reluctant writers to hone their craft using the free web tool's authentic digital format. This is one website that you may find your students want to return to on their own, just to create more stories.

Four Cs

Communication
Critical Thinking
Creativity
Collaboration

ISTE Standards

Creativity and Innovation
Technology Operations
Digital Citizenship
Critical Thinking
Research and Information
Communication and Collaboration

DOK

Level 1—Recall
Level 2—Skills/Concepts
Level 3—Strategic Thinking
Level 4—Extended Thinking

SAMR

Substitution
Augmentation
Modification
Redefinition

goo.gl/ddOFb8

How to Design

- Before creating a story, encourage your students to read other stories and poetry on Storybird.com in order for them to figure out how to create a story themselves.

- There are three options for setting up an account: students can create a Storybird account on Storybird's website, you can set up a class account, or students can sign in with their Google Apps for Education accounts.

- Allow students to play with Storybird first, giving them an opportunity to figure out for themselves how to insert images, add pages, and save their work.

How to Deliver

Link to Storybird in the HyperDoc for students and briefly describe your writing expectations. Allow the "how" to happen on its own, though. Storybird is a simple web tool to figure out, and allowing students to do it themselves builds their confidence for future projects.

How to Collect

For Storybird, we've found it's helpful to demonstrate for students how to find the link to their published work. Provide students with a link to the Google Form so they can turn in their piece's link and view everyone else's published work as well. Ask that students keep their writing public so it can be viewed in the Storybird Gallery.

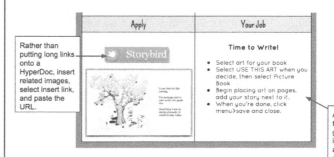

Share

As you design your HyperDoc, think about how your students will share their final products. If you go the traditional route, students show their work in front of the class, with their parents, or within a small group. You could also print students' work and display it either in the classroom or as a gallery walk. If you opt for transformational sharing, students receive feedback from an audience that goes beyond their classmates, teacher, and parents and includes the public. This elevates the sharing experience and gives students a purpose and real audience, which typically increases the quality of work they turn in and promotes an intrinsic motivation to create something awesome so they can get comments, likes, hearts, and similar feedback from the public.

Share Tool: Commenting in Google Docs

We all regularly ask our colleagues for feedback about our ideas, and just as our peers' comments help us grow as learners, they can help our students, too. That's why it's so important to teach students this practice early on. Fortunately, Google has made digital collaboration simple through its apps' sharing and comments features. Simply ask students to share their work via Google Apps and solicit feedback from a classmate (or two or three) using the HyperDoc. This exercise gives students a real audience while also teaching digital citizenship.

In the sample HyperDoc, students are asked to read their classmate's thinking before getting together to have a face-to-face conversation. This preparation allows them to have a more in-depth discussion and use class time efficiently.

Four Cs

Communication
Critical Thinking
Creativity
Collaboration

ISTE Standards

Creativity and Innovation
Technology Operations
Digital Citizenship
Critical Thinking
Research and Information
Communication and Collaboration

DOK

Level 1—Recall
Level 2—Skills/Concepts
Level 3—Strategic Thinking
Level 4—Extended Thinking

SAMR

Substitution
Augmentation
Modification
Redefinition

How to Design

- Create a blended learning environment where students can ...... share their work in person and digitally.
- Offer opportunities to engage in partnerships.
- Invite students to read one another's work in Google Docs and insert thoughtful comments.

How to Deliver

- Share the HyperDoc with students.
- Assign students partners with whom to share their Docs.
- Each partner will read and make comments on the other's work and then return the work to its owner so the owner can read the comments.
- Students comment on classmate's work as appropriate.
- You may have to give students examples of effective comments (digital citizenship, effective partnership lessons).

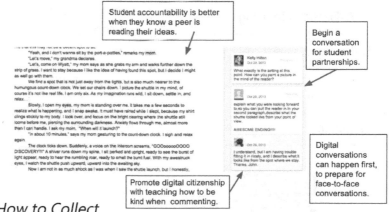

How to Collect

Have students click Share to give you viewing and editing rights to their HyperDocs. This also allows you to collect their comments whenever you need to.

Share Tool: Google Slides

When it comes to selecting a method for sharing student work, sometimes less really is more. Take, for example, Google Slides. Use this tool to get students collaborating and communicating. This simple tool allows students to choose their slides' images, text, videos, links, and graphic designs with little workflow effort. Once a presentation is complete, students can explore one another's work instantly, learning from the content and gaining inspiration for their own designs. Students can also share their completed slide decks through a link or by embedding it into a Google Site, giving an even greater audience the opportunity to explore their work. Working together on one slide deck takes cooperation and is a great opportunity for students to exhibit good digital citizenship.

Four Cs

Communication
Critical Thinking
Creativity
Collaboration

ISTE Standards

Creativity and Innovation
Technology Operations
Digital Citizenship
Critical Thinking
Research and Information
Communication and Collaboration

DOK

Level 1–Recall
Level 2–Skills/Concepts
Level 3—Strategic Thinking
Level 4–Extended Thinking

SAMR

Substitution
Augmentation
Modification
Redefinition

goo.gl/yhFDPl

How to Design

Create a new Google Slides deck through your Google Drive. Adjust the share settings to "Anyone with a link can edit" while the project is in process, allowing you to control the design as much or as little as you need. For example, you could create one slide for each student, add a template for scaffolded instructions, or even add students' names to avoid confusion when selecting a slide to work on.

How to Deliver

Attach a link for a Google Slides presentation directly to a HyperDoc, along with instructions for the project. Since multiple students will be working on the document at one time, it's helpful to keep the slide deck open on your device so you can monitor their progress. You could even project the slide deck in progress onto a screen in the room for instructional purposes, such as to clarify instructions, teach a new design technique, or just showcase clever work.

How to Collect

Once students have completed their slides, set the presentation to view-only to avoid any further changes being made. Share a link to the slide deck as a QR code, through an email, or by embedding it on a website for easy access.

Share Tool: Google Slides

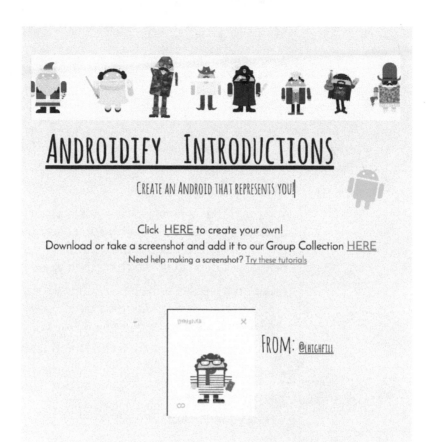

Share Tool: Student Film Festival

The primary reason we have students share their work is to provide them with an authentic audience, a group of people to help students share, grow, and celebrate their ideas. *Hosting a student film festival will help your lessons reach redefinition, because all four Cs will be implemented in highly engaging ways and will culminate with a live audience.* To prepare for the film festival, have students produce films with a real purpose: to share their film's messages with a live or digital audience beyond the classroom. This alone increases students' levels of intrinsic motivation.

The student film festival we describe in the following example uses a blended learning model, with a live event held at a local venue and a digital event online where students can log in and view films. When we hosted our film festival, we curated media resources and the students' films using the HyperDoc website. Here's a sample website with details about our film festival: pusdfilmfestival.weebly.com.

Four Cs

Communication
Critical Thinking
Creativity
Collaboration

ISTE Standards

Creativity and Innovation
Technology Operations
Digital Citizenship
Critical Thinking
Research and Information
Communication and Collaboration

DOK

Level 1—Recall
Level 2—Skills/Concepts
Level 3—Strategic Thinking
Level 4—Extended Thinking

SAMR

Substitution
Augmentation
Modification
Redefinition

How to Design

You can design a film festival event in many ways: with your own class; as a grade level, department, or school; within the community; or open to the public online. How you design and plan your festival will depend on which method you choose.

- Design a website to help you curate your film festival's resources, including video examples, rules, categories, deadlines, support resources, etc.
- Set a deadline and share festival information with participants.
- Invite an audience and publicize your event.
- Prepare the venue.
- Host your film festival!

How to Deliver

Curate all media resources on a website (see sample website at pusdfilmfestival.weebly.com/). This will make it easier for you, your colleagues, and your students to follow along with the rules, deadlines, etc. Students will go to the HyperDoc site to access festival information and eventually share their films. Walk your students through the video production process, encourage them to produce films about their personal passions, and eventually this will help them prepare to enter their work into the festival. Films can be made in class, at home, or both.

Share Tool: Student Film Festival

goo.gl/oT0V2S

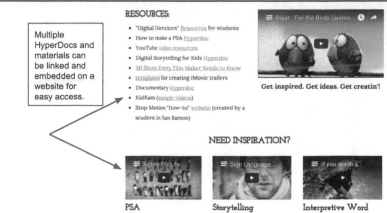

Multiple HyperDocs and materials can be linked and embedded on a website for easy access.

How to Collect

Students can submit their films through a Google Form, which you can link to the website where the other resources are curated. The film festival committee (made up of teachers, student leaders, administrators, etc.) can then access the spreadsheet and begin to judge the video submissions. And who knows? Perhaps all of the videos will be accepted to the film festival.

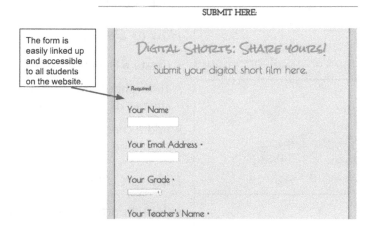

The form is easily linked up and accessible to all students on the website.

Sharing the Films with an Authentic Audience: (This might include the class, school, community, or public online.)

- Curate the student-created films in a YouTube playlist.
- Invite students and their families to a public venue to participate in the film festival.
- Play the students' films on a large screen for the entire community audience to enjoy together.
- Watch your students beam with pride as their films are shared on the big screen!

Share Tool: Digital Portfolios

Students love showing their friends and family members their best work, and a digital portfolio allows them to do just that with a click of their mouse. Instead of filing away projects in a box, only to be tucked away in a garage and never looked at again, digital portfolios showcase a student's learning progression. Families can easily access a digital portfolio, time and time again, to revisit student work when it is linked online and packaged on a digital portfolio.

Google Slides, Sites, and Blogger are all great platforms for students to publish their projects. Help students set up their digital portfolio's organization, purpose, and structure, and chances are, they will continue to build it long after they leave your classroom. This sample HyperDoc includes the guidelines for a class to personalize their work from an entire school year by creating a Google Site.

Four Cs

Communication
Critical Thinking
Creativity
Collaboration

ISTE Standards

Creativity and Innovation
Technology Operations
Digital Citizenship
Critical Thinking
Research and Information
Communication and Collaboration

DOK

Level 1—Recall
Level 2—Skills/Concepts
Level 3—Strategic Thinking
Level 4—Extended Thinking

SAMR

Substitution
Augmentation
Modification
Redefinition

goo.gl/cJjunP   goo.gl/EF0nj8

How to Design

In the HyperDoc, include the following:

- Video tutorials for building a digital portfolio
- A personalized checklist of projects to include
- A Google Form to turn in completed work
- Guidelines for publishing work
- An opportunity for students to reflect on the pieces they chose to include.

How to Deliver

- Create a HyperDoc with a list of steps.
- Throughout the year, use rubrics to promote quality student-created digital content.
- Add a checklist to the HyperDoc to keep track of what projects should be showcased.

How to Collect

- Collect portfolio URLs in a Google Form.

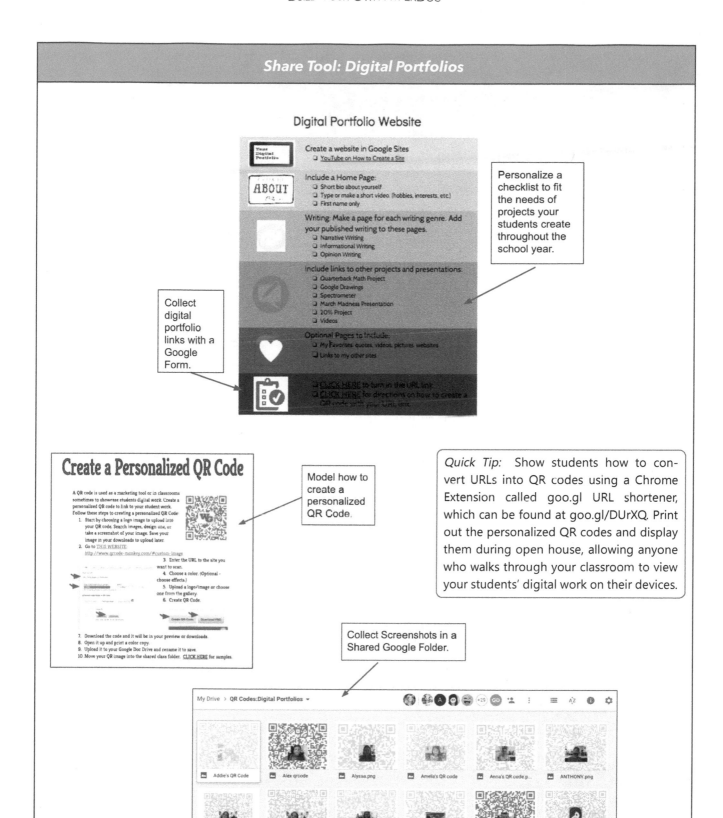

Share Tool: Digital Portfolios

Digital Portfolio Website

Personalize a checklist to fit the needs of projects your students create throughout the school year.

Collect digital portfolio links with a Google Form.

Model how to create a personalized QR Code.

Quick Tip: Show students how to convert URLs into QR codes using a Chrome Extension called goo.gl URL shortener, which can be found at goo.gl/DUrXQ. Print out the personalized QR codes and display them during open house, allowing anyone who walks through your classroom to view your students' digital work on their devices.

Collect Screenshots in a Shared Google Folder.

Share Tool: Google Forms and Spreadsheets

When you have a lot to accomplish and not enough time to do it all, maximizing face time with students is important. So rather than having every student present their individual projects one at a time while the rest of the class passively listens, have your class share their creations digitally.

To do this, provide students with links to both the Google Form and the spreadsheet that has links to all of the projects. Students can then choose which presentations they view and when, having an entire classroom of students with whom to engage and review their peers' projects at one time.

Four Cs

Communication
Critical Thinking
Creativity
Collaboration

ISTE Standards

Creativity and Innovation
Technology Operations
Digital Citizenship
Critical Thinking
Research and Information
Communication and Collaboration

DOK

Level 1—Recall
Level 2—Skills/Concepts
Level 3—Strategic Thinking
Level 4—Extended Thinking

SAMR

Substitution
Augmentation
Modification
Redefinition

goo.gl/J8XAVg

How to Design

In your HyperDoc, attach a Google Form to a prompt like in the example.

- Create a Google Form, being sure to copy the link from the live form.

- Highlight the word "HERE" and insert the link.

- Follow the same instructions for sharing the spreadsheet and setting the share settings as view-only.

How to Deliver

Students can turn in their work using the link in the HyperDoc. Be sure to share any expectations you may have for viewing projects.

How to Collect

Collect your students' work using a Google Form, which creates a spreadsheet that can be shared even outside your classroom.

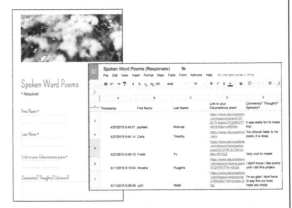

Reflect

"We do not learn from experience ... we learn from reflecting on experience," said John Dewey, an American philosopher, psychologist, and educational reformer. After challenging students to explore, create, and communicate ideas in a HyperDoc, give them an opportunity to reflect on what they've learned, to evaluate their work using rubrics and checklists, and to set new learning goals. Promoting this growth mindset starts by helping them first identify the steps they take when learning something. This could be done as a class discussion or by using a HyperDoc to capture student thinking. However you choose to lead students through the reflection process, though, they must think about two things:

1. How they learned.

2. The academic content—the "what"—they learned using a standard, mandated, or self-created rubric. These rubrics and checklists are generally used for report cards or mandated reporting of student progress, but are helpful to students when they're reflecting on their progress as well.

You can personalize a HyperDoc's reflection section to fit your students' individual goals and meet your district's requirements.

Reflect Tool: Padlet

In your HyperDoc, link to a Padlet (Padlet.com). Padlet is a web tool described as a graffiti wall, online paper, or a digital bulletin board. Teachers can use it to encourage online conversations or quickly collect student thinking.

Four Cs

Communication
Critical Thinking
Creativity
Collaboration

ISTE Standards

Creativity and Innovation
Technology Operations
Digital Citizenship
Critical Thinking
Research and Information
Communication and Collaboration

DOK

Level 1—Recall
Level 2—Skills/Concepts
Level 3—Strategic Thinking
Level 4—Extended Thinking

SAMR

Substitution
Augmentation
Modification
Redefinition

goo.gl/mcLtNs

How to Design

Create a Padlet. Add your questions to the heading and share the link to the Padlet using a shortened URL or link it directly to another HyperDoc.

Create a list of reflective questions that prompt students to think about their role in the learning process. For best results, we recommend generating reflective questions from one or all three of the following categories:

Content: Ask the student about what he learned. Use a broad, theme-based question.

- Who? What? Where? When? Why?
- How does this connect to what we learned?

Personal: Ask about the student•s individual learning experience.

- What part of this assignment was difficult for you? Why?
- How might you approach an activity like this differently next time?
- How did you contribute to your group•s overall effectiveness?

Collaborative: Ask about the group learning experience and his interactions with his partner.

- What did your group do well together?
- How did you support your partner today?
- How did your group problem solve when there were varying points of view?

How to Deliver

At the end of a learning experience, direct students to the Padlet and ask them to record their thinking. Watch the magic unfold as all the thinking in the room is shared in this one live document.

Reflect Tool: Padlet

> Post 3 reflective questions in the heading. Participants type their name in the red heading line and responses below.

 Reflection
1 new understanding 1 best resource 1 celebration/appreciation

1. Having a good template for recording conferring notes is crucial.

2. Workshop Resources Links

3. I appreciate our wonderful instructional coaches.

I really appreciate being with colleagues who are committed to this model. I loved all the connections I made today (technology, resources, problem solving.) I like having a goal - or focus,

the best resource is your resource page

and the coaches.

Celebration of all the work that went

into organizing this day.

Kelly

I'm really wanting to to educate parents about Reader's Workshop. I'm thinking about making my own video to post.

New Resource: Woodburn Units of study for Reader's Workshop

I appreciate everyone's enthusiasm and feel comfortable being with like minded colleagues!

Beth

I have a better understanding about conferring in Reader's Workshop in Kindergarten. I loved the resources and all of the links to check out! I appreciate everyone's great attitude as we dive into the workshop models. It is just great teaching and I am excited that we are focusing on it as a district. Woo hoo!

Leslee

New understanding is that we are all learning and growing no matter what stage of the process you're at. We're all learners

Cynthia

I learned about some awesome literature to help launch

my Small Moments unit.

Reflect Tool: Wordle

The free word clouds created by Wordle (Wordle.net) may initially look like just beautiful collections of words on a page, but when you discuss a word cloud with your students, it can lead to deep, complex reflection. Wordle varies the sizes of words based on how many times they're repeated within the document, which makes analyzing why one word is larger than the others a great place to begin a reflection lesson. Depending on what you asked to generate the words, students can look for patterns, share predictions, and make connections to an assignment's content. Using this method of reflection for team building, to review a concept, or to explore a topic provides students with an opportunity to develop higher-level thinking skills.

Four Cs

Communication
Critical Thinking
Creativity
Collaboration

ISTE Standards

Creativity and Innovation
Technology Operations
Digital Citizenship
Critical Thinking
Research and Information
Communication and Collaboration

DOK

Level 1—Recall
Level 2—Skills/Concepts
Level 3—Strategic Thinking
Level 4—Extended Thinking

SAMR

Substitution
Augmentation
Modification
Redefinition

goo.gl/8nmMG1

How to Design

As you create a question or prompt to generate a set of words around a topic, think about its possible answers and whether or not they would result in a word cloud worthy of rich examination. You can package this portion of your lesson with clear instructions in a HyperDoc.

How to Collect and Deliver:

An easy way to collect words that will populate a Wordle is through a Google Form.

- Attach a link to the form in your HyperDoc. You can then highlight and copy all of the words in the form's spreadsheet at once.

- Open Wordle and, following the website's instructions, paste the text in the designated location.

- Change the Wordle's fonts, color, and shape to achieve your desired look and then either download the image or take a screenshot to share in a location so all participants can access it.

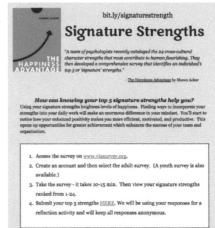

Part 2- Create a Wordle from the responses you gathered in the form. (video tutorial) Share the Wordle with the group as a way to reflect on the strengths and skills each member of the group brings to their job/classroom.

Reflect Tool: Tables in a Google Doc

A popular reflection project is "20% Time." This type of comprehensive project offers students a great opportunity to try new things, explore new topics, take risks, practice time management, and pursue their personal passions. Each week, students work on projects of their choosing, pushing toward a goal and researching ideas. As students work, you provide coaching and feedback. Afterward, students jot notes and reflect on their learning process. And though 20% Time projects are open-ended, you'll be surprised by what your students can do when they have a purpose, an audience, and an opportunity to create.

Four Cs

Communication
Critical Thinking
Creativity
Collaboration

ISTE Standards

Creativity and Innovation
Technology Operations
Digital Citizenship
Critical Thinking
Research and Information
Communication and Collaboration

DOK

Level 1—Recall
Level 2—Skills/Concepts
Level 3—Strategic Thinking
Level 4—Extended Thinking

SAMR

Substitution
Augmentation
Modification
Redefinition

goo.gl/FY4SSd
Entire HyperDoc Assignment:
goo.gl/Hh588r

How to Design

- Insert a table in a Doc.
- Post reflective questions in the table.
- After each weekly work session, give students a chance to reflect on the table on the HyperDoc.

How to Deliver

- Give students time to respond to the questions each week.
- Read the students' responses and offer immediate feedback, asking questions to push thinking, providing resources (as needed), making connections with mentors, and offering motivation.

How to Collect

This HyperDoc can be shared through Google Classroom, allowing you to provide consistent feedback and follow along with your students' progress as they document their work each week.

20% Time Progress Reflection

Each **FRIDAY**, you will have time in class to work on your project. On Fridays, bring in the materials that you will need to work on your project. I will be conferring with you and helping you along. Be aware that your project may evolve over time. If it changes, or you have a new or different idea, please let me know. I will be asking you to report on your progress of your project each week. Use this document to report your progress and to communicate with me about how your project is evolving. When you complete a project, you need to present the project to the class.

Check in weekly on a Google Doc. Keep track on weekly progress and teachers give feedback in the comments section.

Date:	What did you do this week in order to work towards your project goal?	What can I do to support you this week?	On a scale of 1-4, rate how well you worked towards your project goal. Include why you gave yourself this grade.

Reflect Tool: Google Docs

As you design your HyperDoc, think carefully about how you will evaluate your students' learning and how that evaluation process will fit the standards mandated for your classroom. One method you may consider is using rubrics and checklists, which can be embedded into a HyperDoc.

Four Cs

Communication
Critical Thinking
Creativity
Collaboration

ISTE Standards

Creativity and Innovation
Technology Operations
Digital Citizenship
Critical Thinking
Research and Information
Communication and Collaboration

DOK

Level 1—Recall
Level 2—Skills/Concepts
Level 3—Strategic Thinking
Level 4—Extended Thinking

SAMR

Substitution
Augmentation
Modification
Redefinition

goo.gl/fjT8py

How to Design

Insert a rubric or checklist into the HyperDoc. On the Google Doc, make a second copy of the rubric or checklist. The purpose of this is so that both the student and the teacher have a space to reflect on the same HyperDoc.

How to Deliver

Allow students time to record their thinking in the HyperDoc. While your students are reflecting, teachers complete the same exercise and afterward offer students feedback for each student on their individual HyperDoc.

How to Collect

Share the HyperDoc and your students' reflections on the learning process from start to finish with parents and administrators so that they can see student growth.

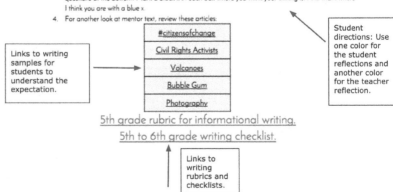

Reflect Tool: Google Docs

Informational Writing Checklist		Not Yet	Starting to	Yes
Structure				
Overall	I used different kinds of information to teach about the subject. Sometimes I included little essays, stories, or "how-to" sections in my writing.			
Lead	I wrote an introduction that helped readers get interested in and understand the subject. I let readers know the subtopics I would be developing later as well as the sequence.			
Transitions	When I wrote about results, I used words and phrases like consequently, as a result, and because of this. When I compared information, I used words and phrases such as in contrast, by comparison, and especially. In narrative parts, I used phrases that go with stories such as a little later and three hours later. In the sections that stated an opinion, I used words such as but the most important reason, for example, and consequently.			
Ending	I wrote a conclusion in which I restated the main points and may have offered a final thought or question for readers to consider.			
Organization	I organized my writing into a sequence of separate sections. I may have used headings and subheadings to highlight the separate sections.			
	I wrote each section according to an organizational plan shaped partly by the genre of the section.			

Writing Checklist copied from district adopted curriculum.

Students, please complete the questions below. Answer as completely and as honestly as you can. Please try to be specific by using the language of the writer's checklist.

As a writer, I did well at....	As a writer, I need to work on....

Students answer reflective questions after completing the checklist.

As your teacher, I will provide feedback here. Your final grade will be posted on this assignment in Google Classroom.

As a writer, I think the student is doing well at....	As a writer, I think the student needs to work on....

Teachers give feedback on the same document. This shared reflective document is easily shared with parents as well!

Reflect Tool: Unit of Study Reflection Slide Deck

For this sample HyperDoc, we created a Google Presentations slide deck to guide our students through the reflection process after they completed a literature unit. You can, however, copy and modify our slide deck to reflect your subject area and unit. Building in time to reflect and capture your students' thoughts in this HyperDoc will help them develop a growth mindset, provide concrete documentation of their reflection as a learner, and set new goals. Preparing for parent-teacher conferences? Let students take full ownership and allow them to facilitate a student-led conference using this HyperDoc.

Four Cs

Communication
Critical Thinking
Creativity
Collaboration

ISTE Standards

Creativity and Innovation
Technology Operations
Digital Citizenship
Critical Thinking
Research and Information
Communication and Collaboration

DOK

Level 1—Recall
Level 2—Skills/Concepts
Level 3—Strategic Thinking
Level 4—Extended Thinking

SAMR

Substitution
Augmentation
Modification
Redefinition

goo.gl/dpscRz

How to Design

Create a new slide deck or use the template we've provided, personalizing the questions to reflect your study unit's specific learning objectives.

How to Deliver

Allow students time to record their thinking in the HyperDoc, which might take multiple class periods. You can give feedback digitally or face-to-face. Also, students can share, read, and reflect with one another.

How to Collect

Use the student work collected in this HyperDoc as a learning assessment. Based on your students' responses, where will you take them next?

What is one CHALLENGE you have faced as a reader?

Describe it here: Insert an image to show how you felt:

Extend

"I'm done—now what do I do?"
"I already know how to do this."
"I learned this last year."
"I'm bored."

At some point, we've all heard at least one of these comments in our classrooms. That's because when we work with such a diverse group of students with varying interests, achievement levels, and pacing needs, we often struggle to keep *all* of our students engaged cognitively *all* of the time. Fortunately, one of the benefits of a HyperDoc is that we can extend our lessons by tagging on "extension ideas" for the students who finish quickly, need an exciting nudge to stay motivated, and willingly accept challenges on their own. This portion of a HyperDoc also gives you the freedom to work one-on-one with those students who need a little more time or support from you while the rest of the class moves ahead and stays on topic.

Once students finish an assignment, you'll find that they will often want to go back and use more web tools from the extend section, allowing them to continue creating—and further their learning. In a HyperDoc, the extension activities are a great way to fit in fun activities that you may never seem to have time for, such as art and design thinking.

There are several ways to extend an assignment or offer extended learning opportunities in a HyperDoc. We've categorized them into four basic types: online games, daily wonderings, progress monitoring, and digital artifacts.

Extend Tool: Online Games

To keep students on topic, engaged, and learning even after they have completed an assignment, link to an online game like Smarty Pins (smartypins.withgoogle.com) in your HyperDoc.

Four Cs

Communication
Critical Thinking
Creativity
Collaboration

ISTE Standards

Creativity and Innovation
Technology Operations
Digital Citizenship
Critical Thinking
Research and Information
Communication and Collaboration

DOK

Level 1—Recall
Level 2—Skills/Concepts
Level 3—Strategic Thinking
Level 4—Extended Thinking

SAMR

Substitution
Augmentation
Modification
Redefinition

goo.gl/WvcJC8

How to Design

If you are simply linking students to an online game, you most likely will not need to design anything from scratch. Instead, choose from the multitude of engaging games already available. Simply select one that is content and age appropriate and add a link to it in your HyperDoc.

How to Deliver

In your HyperDoc, link students directly to the online games for extra practice in class. Your HyperDoc may look like our sample once the link is in place.

How to Collect

You probably won't have to worry about collecting student work from the extend portion of your HyperDoc, especially if your students are simply playing online games.

A simple heading and directions will draw students in!

Finished Early?
Click **HERE** to play Smarty Pins!!
Fun geography guessing game!

Google Maps
SMARTY P**I**NS
PUTTING TRIVIA ON THE MAP

After completing a geography activity on Google Maps, this is the perfect online activity to link up - related to the content but also fun for students to play!

Extend Tool: *Wonderopolis*

As twenty-first-century teachers, it's our job to find the most engaging, relevant, and meaningful websites that will encourage our students' creativity. Wonderopolis (Wonderopolis.org) is one of the best.

This educational resource updates daily, keeping students on topic, engaged in exploring a subject, and wondering (and learning). Wonderopolis is the type of website you'll want to include in your HyperDoc as an extension activity and one that students will revisit independently long after the lesson is complete.

Four Cs

Communication
Critical Thinking
Creativity
Collaboration

ISTE Standards

Creativity and Innovation
Technology Operations
Digital Citizenship
Critical Thinking
Research and Information
Communication and Collaboration

DOK

Level 1—Recall
Level 2—Skills/Concepts
Level 3—Strategic Thinking
Level 4—Extended Thinking

SAMR

Substitution
Augmentation
Modification
Redefinition

goo.gl/hy2LIY

How to Design

There is not necessarily a design element with Wonderopolis; instead, determine how you want to encourage your students to use the website. Students could:

- Search for a "wonder" (as it is referred to on the website) about a particular topic.

- Choose an interactive wonder from the Wonder Jar to share with their families. (This would be fun homework!)

- Do a hands-on Maker lesson

- Add their own question or wonder to the Wonder Bank.

How to Deliver

In your HyperDoc, direct students or link to Wonderopolis.org.

How to Collect

Discuss interesting things students have learned by reading other people's wonders and answers on Wonderopolis' website. Foster a culture of wondering in your classroom by creating a physical jar for students to put their wonders in. This collection of wonders can launch future individual research topics or class discussions.

You can be creative in how you title your "Extend" section.

Simple, clear, engaging directions with the website link embedded.

Wanna Keep Travelin'??

Click HERE to visit Wonderopolis.

Using the Search Tool, type in a place you're curious about, and let the traveling and wondering begin!

Extend Tool: Google Blogger

If you truly want to create an extension experience for your students, then consider setting up a blog for your class using a web tool like Google Blogger (Blogger.com). With a little encouragement from you, the blog becomes a creative outlet where students will continually go to jot down their favorite thoughts, quotes, and images about a topic, extending the learning process beyond the lesson. *When students share their blog posts with one another and know that they will receive feedback from a broader audience, they are motivated to write better-quality pieces. Going public with blogs helps to redefine the learning experience.*

In our sample HyperDoc, you'll see how Blogger, or any blogging tool for that matter, allows your students to extend their reading comprehension even after you've taught a skill or strategy.

Four Cs

Communication
Critical Thinking
Creativity
Collaboration

ISTE Standards

Creativity and Innovation
Technology Operations
Digital Citizenship
Critical Thinking
Research and Information
Communication and Collaboration

DOK

Level 1—Recall
Level 2—Skills/Concepts
Level 3—Strategic Thinking
Level 4—Extended Thinking

SAMR

Substitution
Augmentation
Modification
Redefinition

goo.gl/4hP2Wc

How to Design

Designing your blog can be easy or complex, depending on how many bells and whistles you want to include, but the basics are a header, body, and sidebar. Students can draft a new post anytime, and Blogger will archive it chronologically. You can also organize content onto pages, offering you and your students even more flexibility. Students will use elements of graphic design to enhance their blog, consider their readers, and showcase their personalities!

- Create a blog on Blogger.

- Customize your template.

- Start posting.

- Ask students to turn in and share their posts with their peers. Depending on the age/grade level, students might post individually, or teachers will approve/post for them.

- Students read and comment on classmates' posts.

How to Deliver

You can introduce blogs at any point in the year, but making it an extension activity early on will let you get more mileage out of it. You can structure the content, allow it to be freeform so students can express themselves, or some variation of both by providing guidelines for students but letting them choose the content and structure.

Extend Tool: Google Blogger

How to Collect

Collect the link to each student's blog once, and you'll have it forever. We recommend using a Google Form to collect the links so you can access them anytime in a spreadsheet.

As a side note, one of the benefits of designing a blog as a yearlong extension activity is that you can monitor a student's progress by using tags and checking their archived posts. Students will draft posts throughout the year, allowing you to see their growth in a very concrete way. You could even share students' links with their peers, so they can hold one another accountable for maintaining quality posts, and with parents so they can celebrate their child's growth. Blogs are not only a great extension activity for your students, but also an insightful yearlong assessment for you!

You can create a "table of contents" for your HyperDoc to keep students focused on the parts of your Unit of Study.

Extend Tool: Canva

Canva is an online graphic design platform. It offers free access to a wide assortment of design tools and options that encourage creativity. Students can extend a lesson concept by graphically designing an artifact on Canva.

Four Cs

Communication
Critical Thinking
Creativity
Collaboration

ISTE Standards

Creativity and Innovation
Technology Operations
Digital Citizenship
Critical Thinking
Research and Information
Communication and Collaboration

DOK

Level 1—Recall
Level 2—Skills/Concepts
Level 3—Strategic Thinking
Level 4—Extended Thinking

SAMR

Substitution
Augmentation
Modification
Redefinition

goo.gl/FBvQeP

How to Design

Canva (Canva.com) offers wonderful design tutorials so both you and your students can learn the basics of design in addition to more advanced skills and techniques. Use Canva to design something from scratch or choose from the website's incredible library of templates for everything from posters to magazines and infographics. Canva even offers materials so you can teach the basics of graphic design in your classroom.

How to Deliver

As with any HyperDoc extension activity, simply add a link to Canva's website and a few simple directions for students.

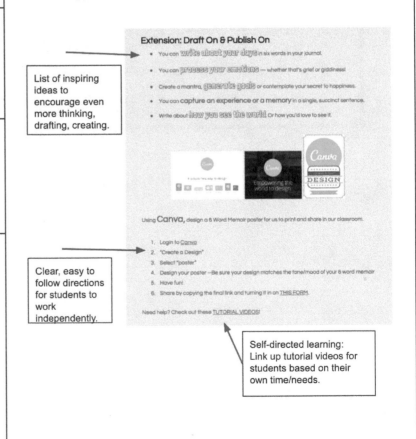

List of inspiring ideas to encourage even more thinking, drafting, creating.

Clear, easy to follow directions for students to work independently.

Self-directed learning: Link up tutorial videos for students based on their own time/needs.

Extend Tool: Canva

Quick Tip: Direct students to the Canva Design School (designschool.canva.com), where they will find video tutorials to quickly transform their graphic design skills! (You'll want to visit this resource yourself, too.) https://goo.gl/nNLREn

How to Collect

You can collect students' Canva designs a number of ways. Students can do the following:

- Download their Canva design directly and turn it in.
- Take a screenshot of it and add it to their social media site, digital portfolio, etc.
- Email or share it with themselves, you, or their classmates, etc.
- Turn in a link to it using a Google Form, Padlet, etc.

How to Use the Templates

Now that you've learned how to create a HyperDoc, let the templates offer a foundation as you create your own HyperDocs and help raise the level of your digital lesson planning. Allow these templates to serve as a starting point, offering ideas and inspiration.

To start designing your HyperDocs, select the template that best fits your classroom, make a copy, and begin customizing it. Apply your content, add images, change fonts, edit text, and adjust other design elements so that the template fits your lesson plans. In short, make the template your own. After you're familiar with our templates, you can move on to creating original HyperDocs without the need for a template.

We have included different templates as well as a sample created using that particular template. Some of these templates are meant to be "one-and-done lessons" that take forty-five to sixty minutes, while others are units of study that will take more than two days to implement. We wanted to share a variety of options so that you can find one that fits your needs—your content, your students, your ideal lesson design.

We've included these templates:
- Basic HyperDoc Template
- Explore-Explain-Apply
- Workshop Model
- Five Es Model
- Five Es Model—Hero's Journey

Visit **HyperDocs.co/templates** to download any of these templates.

TEMPLATE: Basic HyperDoc Lesson

TITLE
Brief Description/Outcome

Engage
{insert video, quote, other inspirational hook}

Explore
{insert instructional video, multimedia text sets, etc.}

Explain
{insert tool for students to collaborate on ideas}

Apply
{insert space for students to create, draft, etc.}

Share
{tool to create something, assessment evidence}

Reflect
{insert enrichment links, extra activities}

Extend
{insert enrichment links, extra activities}

SAMPLE: Creative Writing Challenge

Creative Writing Challenge

Engage

"Good Writing is Hard Work"
Is this true for you?

Turn to the person next to you and discuss why or why not.

Explore

Go to:
storybird.com
Sign in using your Google Account.

Read others stories
Click here to explore.

Explain

Class lesson:
review the components of a well crafted story.

Apply

 Time to Write!

- Begin placing art on pages, add your story next to it.
- When you're done, click menu>save and close.

TEMPLATE: Explore-Explain-Apply

Title

Explore	Your Task
Insert links, images, videos, or articles which allow students to independently build background knowledge for a topic.	Add instructions, guiding questions, or expectations for their exploration.
Explain	**Your Task**
Add video, articles, or pause for a whole group lesson to explain the content.	Post learning expectations for students. Will they take notes? Possibly share their thinking digitally or on paper?
Apply	**Your Task**
Post instructions for the method students will be using to apply their knowledge from the lesson.

Tip: Use images and bullet point steps to simplify the process. | Include expectations for student creations. This could include due dates, links to rubrics, and instructions for turning work in. |

SAMPLE: Animal Reports

ThingLink Animal Reports

Explore	Your Task
★ Making a ThingLink Account

★ Explore different ThingLinks
  ○ Which images made the best ThingLinks?
  ○ What would you want to include in yours? | |
| **Explain** | **Your Task** |
| ★ Learn how to create your own ThingLink.

ThingLink Tutorial | ★ Learn how to find the perfect image for your ThingLink using the Research Tool in Google Docs. |
| **Apply** | **Your Task** |
| ★ Show what you know about your animal using ThingLink. | ★ **Share:** Turn in your ThingLink **HERE**

★ Explore reports **HERE**

★ **Reflect:** As you explore your classmates' ThingLink Reports:
  ○ What do you notice that all animals have in common with each other?
  ○ What makes them different from each other? |

TEMPLATE: Workshop Model

Title of Lesson
Name the "Teaching Point"

Help the writer not the writing

Connection
{insert short video, engaging image}
{YouTube, image, quote, ThingLink}

Teach/Learn
{Face-to-face whole class learning}

Engagement Activity
{insert tool for students to collaborate on ideas}
{Padlet, Google Hangout with another class}

Independent Application
{insert space for students to draft, jot their thinking, create a graphic organizer, or draft in notebooks}
{Docs, Canva, Explain Everything, Educreations, Draw}

Share
{use digital tool to provide an opportunity for partner, small group, or whole class share; Or create an artifact}
{Padlet, Canva, one shared table on Docs, etc.}

SAMPLE: Nonfiction Reading

Challenges in Nonfiction
Readers monitor their own comprehension and notice when they veer off, and use different strategies to get back on track!

Reading is a Journey
Reading is a journey. Sometimes you are cruising along, and sometimes you come to a road block. {video}

Be prepared to say "STOP!" when you don't understand and ask, "What is making this so hard?"
When you notice that you are stuck, you can use a tool to help you!

Know When to Stop!
1. Lay out your text complexity cards with your partner.
2. Listen as I read the text aloud. Be listening to learn.
3. Stop me if there is a part that seems confusing. Hold up your hand like a stop sign.
4. Practice using the complexity cards by naming a way the text gets hard, and then turning the card over to find a strategy.

STOP

Read On ...
1. Read on with your partner, and stop yourselves when you get stuck.
2. Notice and name why that part was tricky for you.
3. Turn your card over to see what strategy you can use to help you.

CAUTION
READ ON ...
With Caution

Lesson adapted from Collins, 5th Grade Unit 2 Teaching Text Complexity, Session #5

TEMPLATE: Five Es Model

SAMPLE: Cellular Respiration, Photosynthesis

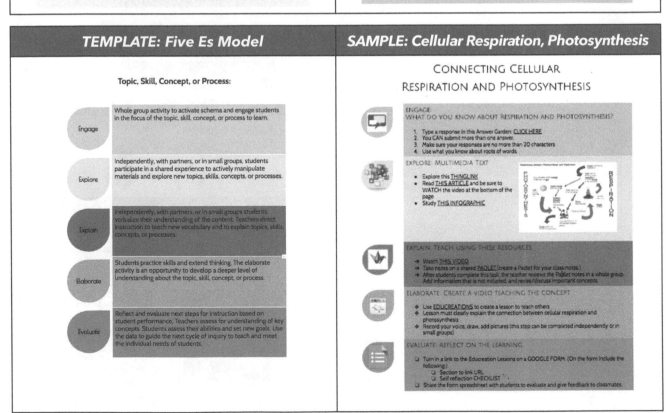

TEMPLATE: Hero's Journey	SAMPLE: Solar Energy

 **Topic X Hyperdoc**

Phase 1: The Call to Adventure

A situation is presented -- designed to spark interest in Topic X (~15 min)

Use Engage tools

Phase 2: Entering the Unknown

A guided challenge is assigned --
requires student to seek answers to their question about Topic X (~45 min)

Use Explore tools

Phase 3: Meeting the Mentor

A tailored lecture is presented where additional informational and tools
related to Tool X are given (~10 min)

Use Explain tools

Phase 4: Transformation

A new challenge task is presented which requires student to apply
understanding of Topic X to a new scenario. (~50 min)

Use Apply Tools

Phase 5: Mastery

A content/skills assessment, private mentor reflection (~45 min)

Use Reflect/Share tools

 **Solar Energy
Around the World:
Solutions in Electricity**

Phase 1: The Call to Adventure ~15 min.

About 1.2 billion people do not have access to electricity.

 YOUR HELP IS NEEDED!

1. Read THIS article.
2. Write one shocking fact from article.
3. With a partner, discuss one of the facts that had an impact on you.

The challenge: How can we harness the power of the sun around the world?

Phase 2: Entering the Unknown ~45 min.

Let's discover ways to bring inexpensive solutions to others!

DISCOVER YOUR SUPERHERO POTENTIAL!

1. Explore this gallery of images and videos about innovative solutions harnessing the sun.
2. Watch this video and then describe the costs involved and supplies needed to develop a solar solution in India. Jot here:
3. Read more about solar power in low-income communities.

Phase 3: Meeting the Mentor ~10 min.

How does solar energy work?
Be thinking, "How can I harness the sun with household energy?"

Let these texts be your "mentor." Read about solar energy to see how you can push yourself to develop a new solution.

1. Energy Now Video   Nat. Geographic Video   Short Film
2. 'Read' this (optional) book.

 **SURFACE AREA REQUIRED TO POWER THE WORLD**

Phase 4: Transformation ~50 min.

Once you create your own electricity with simple household items you will want to transform the world!

GO FOR IT!

With your partner, you will construct your own LITER OF LIGHT!
1. Watch this video for directions
2. Gather materials
3. Build it
4. Reflect on it

Describe the challenges:

Describe the successes:

Phase 5: Mastery ~50 min.

Wear your hero badge and show what you know!

a hero
is an ordinary individual
who finds the strength
to persevere and endure
in spite of
overwhelming obstacles.
- Christopher Reeve

Write a reflection about the experience in building your liter of light. Be sure to think about how "simple" it may have been, but consider how "complex" the problem with electricity seems around the world.

Menu of options to show your new understanding of solar energy:
- Build a circuit for "Liter of Light" - instructional video
- Create your own instructional video
- Create an infographic describing the issues of solar energy in other parts of the world outside of the United States
- Consider a solar solution for ... (you decide!)
- Discover some new solutions that have not been mentioned yet. What household items could you use?

Checklists to Hack Your HyperDocs

To "hack" is to change something in an extraordinary way. Once you become a HyperDoc creator, you might find yourself revising HyperDocs quite often. But if HyperDocs are "The Ultimate Change Agent," how does one know if they are truly changing the student learning experience in an extraordinary way?

We have created an original tool to take HyperDocs from a doc with links to digital lessons that redefine student learning.

Self-assessment and reflection are critical components in teaching and learning. We also believe that these are critical to effective lesson design. The checklist is a resource when you, the lesson designer, are ready to "hack" your own lessons, align your own HyperDocs to different measures, and discover ways to further incorporate technology and the 4 Cs into your classroom.

Remember: Not all HyperDocs will be transformative; some will simply enhance the learning process and are lessons scaffolded in delivery that lead to a redefined experience. Additionally, as professional educators, we understand that student application of DOK levels will vary based on the objectives you have in mind for your individual students. We encourage teachers, instructional coaches, and administrators to use this checklist for trainings, observations and evaluations.

TRANSFORMATION

Checklist to Hack Your HyperDoc

SAMR Tech Integration	DOK Critical Thinking
REDEFINITION *Does your lesson allow for creation of new tasks previously inconceivable?* *Do your students, create, collaborate, or connect beyond the classroom?*	**LEVEL 4** *Does your lesson allow students to engage in high levels of critical thinking?* *Does your lesson offer extended thinking through an investigation, with time to think and process multiple conditions of the problem?*
☐ **CREATE** Students direct video projects, design a project to synthesize information, develop games or websites, and/or demonstrate mastery of a topic. ☐ **COLLABORATE** Create together combining ideas. ☐ **CONNECT** Using teleconferencing tools, connect locally and/or globally, interact on social media, share ideas via public comments, and/or use tools to create social change. ☐ **VOICE and CHOICE** Student driven projects that provide opportunities to develop a skill. ☐ **SHARE** Student work is shared with an authentic audience beyond the classroom and home.	☐ **APPRAISE** Students evaluate their own work or the work of others ☐ **CONNECT** Students connect new ideas with previous ideas ☐ **CRITIQUE/JUDGE** Offer purposeful commentary on the work of others (expert articles, classmates) ☐ **DESIGN** Develop and design authentic investigations, inquiry projects around student ☐ **JUSTIFY/PROVE** Collect and share data and/or opinions to make an argument or statement. ☐ **SYNTHESIZE/REPORT** Share out new, central understandings around a topic
MODIFICATION *Does your lesson allow for significant task redesign?* *How are students using technology to learn how to learn?*	**LEVEL 3** *Does your lesson require strategic thinking?* *Does your lesson offer opportunities for students to reason, develop a plan, or a sequence of steps?*
☐ **EXAMINE** Study multimedia text sets and integrate ideas and/or find themes. ☐ **COMMUNICATE** Use share features to discuss ideas. ☐ **INTERPLAY** Make choices and explore interactive websites through with a variety of link's (games, videos, images, text, etc.) ☐ **INTERACT** Provide feedback and use suggestion features. ☐ **PRACTICE** Students practice developing digital citizenship, visual and/or digital literacy	☐ **CITE EVIDENCE** Support ideas with details and examples. ☐ **DEVELOP** Use voice appropriate to the purpose and audience. ☐ **ASSESS/INVESTIGATE** Identify research questions and design investigations for a specific problem. ☐ **COMPARE/CONTRAST** Determine the author's purpose and describe how it affects the interpretation of a reading selection. ☐ **DIFFERENTIATE** Apply a concept in other contexts.

ENHANCEMENT

Checklist to Hack Your HyperDoc

SAMR Tech Integration	DOK Critical Thinking
AUGMENTATION *Does your lesson plan use tech as a direct tool substitute with functional change?* *Is your lesson scaffolded to build up to a transformative lesson?*	**LEVEL 2** *Does your lesson develop skills leading to a deeper level of critical thinking?* *Do students apply concepts or conceptual knowledge in two or more steps?*
☐ **LITERACY** Read digitally, record thinking, share responses, take notes, and use graphic organizers. ☐ **ASSESS** Collect digital assessments that substitute previously used assessments. ☐ **COPY** Use assignments previously created and copy into Docs. Augment using share features.	☐ **EXTRAPOLATE** Summarize the major events in a digital text. ☐ **FORMULATE** Use context cues to identify the meaning of unfamiliar words ☐ **COMPUTE** Solve routine multiple-step problems. ☐ **CONVERT** Describe the cause/effect Identify patterns in events or behavior. ☐ **DISTINGUISH** Organize, represent and interpret data.
SUBSTITUTION *Does your lesson design act as a direct tool substitute with no functional change?* *Is your lesson teaching foundational skills that will lead to more complex skills?*	**LEVEL 1** *Do your lesson ask students to recall a fact, information, or procedure?* *Does your lesson ask students to process information at a low level?*
☐ **SUBSTITUTE** Copy and paste a PDF worksheet or digital file ☐ **TYPE** Word processing, digital images, fill in the blanks ☐ **DIRECT** Provide directions ☐ **READ** Read digital text	☐ **RECALL** elements and details of story structure, such as sequence of events, character, plot and setting ☐ **NAME** Conduct basic calculations or fill in the blank with options provided. ☐ **MATCH** Vocabulary and definitions. ☐ **RECORD** Label locations on a map. ☐ **ILLUSTRATE** Represent in words or diagrams a concept or relationship.

View the Checklist to Hack Your HyperDoc by scanning the QR code below.

goo.gl/58PJAF

HACK with ISTE

Looking at the ISTE's standards for students, teachers, and coaches, HyperDocs have the potential to meet all of the requirements listed. Use these ISTE standards as either a checklist for professional development or as another assessment tool to reflect on a HyperDoc lesson's design and implementation (Figure 3-2).

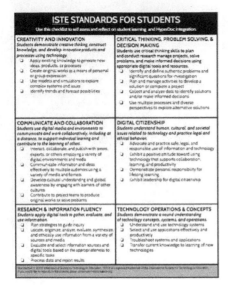
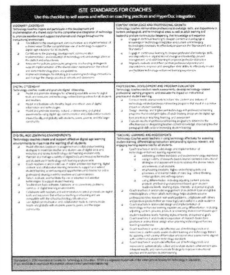

Figure 3-2

View the checklist for ISTE Standards by scanning the QR code below.

goo.gl/Z5tKrn

"...nourishes creativity amongst teachers."

HyperDocs have been a game changer in my science class! The students find the lessons to be a user-friendly way of sharing information with them, and they allow for greater choice. They can choose to work collaboratively on some things, and individually on others. This independence is really important in middle school, as it provides a way for the *students to feel empowered* while also having buy-in to the curriculum at hand.

I would love to see more HyperDocs being created and shared. This serves two purposes. First, *it allows for collaboration among teachers, which is not only a huge time-saver but, also nourishes creativity amongst teachers.*

Second it helps teachers model what we are asking our students to do—come up with something that is meaningful to you while working with others. I think it's so important to continuously grow and expand our craft and to constantly look for ways to support all types of learners. I am starting to teach others at my school, as well as, starting to connect

with others through Twitter and Teachers Give Teachers. *The energy that you experience when collaborating is what drives you to keep creating new and exciting things.*

Tessie Gonsales, @mtgonsalves
science teacher

4
Off You Go!
Final Tips and Advice from Students

So who are we doing all of this for? The students! We are doing this because education has called for a change in the way that we teach. After teaching with HyperDocs for a few years now and reflecting on how they were changing our classrooms, we started to notice the power of designing digital lessons that truly engage students and help them along in their learning progress.

In the chart on the next page, we've summarized two of our favorite articles in an attempt to highlight why we wrote this book: we want to engage our students, and HyperDocs are the solution.

In the left column, we summarize an article called, "Kids Speak Out on Student Engagement," and in the right column is a summary of another article, "Nine Ways to Plan Transformational Lessons: Planning the Best Curriculum Unit Ever." As you begin to design and deliver transformational lessons using your customized HyperDocs, we encourage you to keep this chart close by and listen to the voices of those students speaking out and to the voices of the students in your classroom.

What Kids Want	HyperDoc Solutions
(From Edutopia's Article: Kid's Speak Out on Student Engagem...)	(From Edutopia's Article: 9 Ways to Plan Transformational Lessons: Planning)
Opportunities to work with their peers: • Allow them to collaborate. • Put them in partnerships and groups.	**Shift from solo to collaborative lesson design:** • Reach out to colleagues • Use social media tools as a Professional Learning Community • Share.. Share… Share at @TsGiveTs[3]
To work with technology: • Consume time. • Create time.	**Provide opportunities with your students in mind:** • It's so good that we will repeat it… *voice and choice!* Everyone has one. Allow students to develop a voice. • Write objectives for students (not an administrator) to read
Work that connects them to the real world (Project-Based Learning): • Use digital tools to connect beyond the four walls of your classroom. • Provide a purpose and an audience.	**Create an assessment before developing content** • If using a creation tool for assessment, give students time to play with the tool before they have to use the tool to as an assessment. • Plan backwards so you know where you are going!
For you to clearly love what you do! • Learn and grow with your students! • Celebrate their expertise. • Incorporate time for play! (Thanks to Global School Play Day Committee for making this a priority!)	**Integrate productive struggle into the curriculum:** • Model and expect a growth mindset • Change the narrative from "I don't get it!" to "I don't get it yet, but I will!" • Don't forget the introverts!
The chance to get out of their seats: • Rethink the design and space of your classroom. • Use blended learning strategies to balance student work time. • Include standing tech bars, carpet space, and flexible furniture to promote movement.	**Create presentations that do more showing and less telling:** • A picture is worth a thousand words. • Death by powerpoint! Fewer words. Less teacher talk time. Your students may surprise you with what they know!

1 "Kids Speak Out on Student Engagement." Edutopia." 2012. 17 Jan. 2016
2 "9 Ways to Plan Transformational Lessons. Edutopia." 2014. 4 Feb. 2016
3 "TeachersGiveTeachers (@TsGiveTs) | Twitter." 2015. 17 Jan. 2016

Teachers Give Teachers, a Common Story

We were talking lesson plans with a frustrated new teacher who said she couldn't find good resources for her upcoming unit, and her grade-level team didn't have anything they were willing to share. Later, she told us that she had found a great unit online but had to pay to access the materials. After purchasing the unit, she was shocked and disappointed when she realized the author was one of the teachers on her own team.

That was the turning point when we went to Twitter and created TeachersGiveTeachers (@TsGiveTs), which encourages teachers to share digital lessons for free. In a time when collaboration is touted as an essential skill, it had become clear to us that teachers needed a place where they could experience the power of creating, sharing, and connecting with other like-minded educators, free of judgment and free of cost. This has become the perfect environment for a HyperDoc to thrive in.

Give One, Take One

Since HyperDocs are created using Google Apps, it's easy to make a copy of one and edit it to fit your classroom's needs. Maybe you like the design and layout, but the content doesn't match your grade level. In that case, add your ideas but keep the colors and tables the same. You could also borrow just a section that supports a unit you've created, or even connect with a HyperDoc author and work on a lesson together. Remember, though: if you use someone else's HyperDoc, giving credit to the original author is important, as it not only shows respect for the process, but also for other teachers. Just add "inspired by" or "original design by" at the bottom of the lesson.

If you want to share one of the HyperDocs you've created, make it view-only, take off links to your personal student collection, and mark it with your name. If you share your lesson on Twitter, link to your document in a Tweet and include @TsGiveTs and #HyperDocs.

Better Together

Be sure to visit the Teachers Give Teachers website at **teachersgiveteachers.net** to search for specific HyperDocs and to turn in HyperDocs you wish to share. Teachers who create clever HyperDocs are being showered with replies and likes daily, as their lessons are Retweeted and taking off across the country. It has been powerful witnessing teachers who have never met connect over the theory of good lesson design and bring a new energy to building the craft we love.

HyperDocs were never meant to replace curriculum, but instead to reignite the passion for creating powerful lessons, to bond people who love teaching.

"... real learning is going to happen."

As I create HyperDocs to give students a creative way to express what we are learning in class I find that I am challenged to be creative myself. *When the teacher and students are both stretching themselves creatively, real learning is going to happen.* HyperDocs teach much more than content and classroom information. Students are learning graphic design, teamwork, brainstorming and problem solving. The process then is not just educating a student in a particular subject but really *developing skills that are necessary to be successful in life.*

I regularly post my HyperDocs on Instagram as well as Teachers Give Teachers and check out the work of others. *I love interacting with those across the country* who are continually looking for ways to improve their craft and enrich and empower their students. Twitter has been great for making those connections. Not really able to make many conferences, but when I do there are definitely people I am going to want to sit down and talk with.

Matt MacFarlane, @mrmacsclasses
middle school teacher

Your Journey Begins

We hear our students' call to adventure, "Come engage us!" We recognize the need to inspire and motivate students and to prepare them with skills needed to learn and create in a modern world. As educators, we entered this profession because we have a passion for children, because we believe we can inspire lifelong learners and have a positive effect on their lives. But we don't always know how to do that. In order to respond to our learners and give them exactly what they deserve, HyperDocs were our solution.

Each of us transformed our classrooms to reflect the style of learning we believe our students deserve: students negotiating ideas on a digital project, us working closely with small groups of students while their peers engaged with a HyperDoc, learners sharing their work with others and receiving feedback, and every student gaining an overall sense of pride and purpose. In the process, our students started feeling valued and validated, and we enjoyed learning alongside our students while we designed and delivered HyperDocs. HyperDocs became the answer for how to teach with technology that we'd been searching for.

But this has certainly been a journey, and as with all journeys, we've had our share of ups and downs, including new mandates, financial cutbacks, standardized assessments, and grades to submit. However, we have embraced this journey, and we invite you to do the same.

As educators, we share a passion for teaching. While you're on your personal journey to teach more effectively with technology and transform your own classroom, understand that although the tools will change, pedagogy and good teaching won't. When you need a boost, like we certainly have, enlist the mentorship of your students, your colleagues down the hall, and even educators on social media. When an idea or lesson is going well for you and your students, share it and let your success help more students. And when you're using HyperDocs to enhance your teaching, allow the struggles you face and the success you feel to become a meaningful and "learningful" time in your journey. A change agent works tirelessly, but feels energized as a result. Technology won't be what transforms learning for your students; *it is you*—your courage to try new things and your heart for teaching.

HyperDoc instruction does not have a singular look or feel, but we hope you experience the empowerment and joy that comes from connecting with your students and colleagues throughout your journey, so you, too, can become a change agent, the everyday hero students want.

Want more HyperDocs?

Here are ways to stay connected:

1. Host a Workshop at Your School
- HyperDoc Workshop: Create and Customize Digital Lessons for Your Classroom (one-day)
- Engage Me! How to Create HyperDocs for Student-Centered Classrooms (half-day)
- Private Label—We will customize a workshop to fit your school's needs!

2. Take the Online Course:
- HyperDocs BootCamp

3. Attend a workshop featuring Google for Education in your area

4. Book the HyperDoc Authors for a Keynote

**For more information or to request a workshop
or keynote presentation, visit ElevateBooksEdu.com.**

HyperDocs.co | #HyperDocs | Facebook.com/groups/HyperDocs

More from Elevate Books EDU

ElevateBooksEdu.com/books

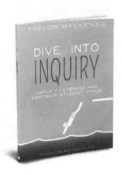

Dive into Inquiry

Amplify Learning and Empower Student Voice
By Trevor MacKenzie

Dive into Inquiry beautifully marries the voice and choice of inquiry with the structure and support required to optimize learning. With Dive into Inquiry you'll gain an understanding of how to best support your learners as they shift from a traditional learning model into the inquiry classroom where student agency is fostered and celebrated each and every day.

Inquiry Mindset

Nurturing the Dreams, Wonders, and Curiosities of Our Youngest Learners
By Trevor MacKenzie and Rebecca Bathurst-Hunt

Inquiry Mindset offers a highly accessible journey through inquiry in the younger years. Learn how to empower your students, increase engagement, and accelerate learning by harnessing the power of curiosity. With practical examples and a step-by-step guide to inquiry, Trevor MacKenzie and Rebecca Bathurst-Hunt make inquiry-based learning simple.

The Google Infused Classroom

A Guidebook to Making Thinking Visible and Amplifying Student Voice
By Holly Clark and Tanya Avrith

This beautifully designed book offers guidance on using technology to design instruction that allows students to show their thinking, demonstrate their learning, and share their work (and voices!) with authentic audiences. *The Google Infused Classroom* will equip you to empower your students to use technology in meaningful ways that prepare them for the future.

Sketchnotes for Educators

100 Inspiring Illustrations for Lifelong Learners
By Sylvia Duckworth

Sylvia Duckworth is a Canadian teacher whose sketchnotes have taken social media by storm. Her drawings provide clarity and provoke dialogue on many topics related to education. This book contains 100 of her most popular sketchnotes with links to the original downloads that can be used in class or shared with colleagues. Interspersed throughout the book are Sylvia's reflections on each drawing and what motivated her to create them, in addition to commentary from other educators who inspired the sketchnotes.

How to Sketchnote

Visual Note-taking Made Easy
By Sylvia Duckworth

Educator and internationally known sketchnoter Sylvia Duckworth makes ideas memorable and shareable with her simple yet powerful drawings. In *How to Sketchnote*, she explains how you can use sketchnoting in the classroom and that you don't have to be an artist to discover the benefits of doodling!

40 Ways to Inject Creativity into Your Classroom with Adobe Spark

By Ben Forta and Monica Burns

Experienced educators Ben Forta and Monica Burns offer step-by-step guidance on how to incorporate this powerful tool into your classroom in ways that are meaningful and relevant. They present 40 fun and practical lesson plans suitable for a variety of ages and subjects as well as 15 graphic organizers to get you started. With the tips, suggestions, and encouragement in this book, you'll find everything you need to inject creativity into your classroom using Adobe Spark.

About the Authors

Lisa Highfill (@lhighfill) is an instructional technology coach in the San Francisco Bay Area. She earned her masters in educational technology leadership and has been a classroom teacher for more than twenty years. As a MERIT fellow, Google Certified Innovator and a YouTube Star Teacher, she travels the globe presenting at EdTech conferences and speaking about lesson design and learning theory.

Kelly Hilton (@kellyihilton) taught in the classroom for fifteen years and is currently an instructional coach in the San Francisco Bay Area of California. She leads professional development on topics such as technology integration, global education, and reading/writing workshop. She is a MERIT fellow and the co-founder of Schoogle Digital Reboot Camp. Kelly is dedicated to collaborating with teachers daily in all subject areas on student-centered instructional design and delivery practices.

Sarah Landis (@sarahlandis) is an instructional coach in the San Francisco Bay Area with more than fifteen years of experience in education. She has a masters in curriculum from Teachers College, Columbia University. She is also a MERIT fellow and the co-founder of Schoogle Digital Reboot Camp. Sarah loves to share her passion for digital literacy, global citizenship, curriculum design, and blended learning with learners of all ages!